UNITY LIBRARY & ARCHIVES
Study in Hosea.
BS 580 H6 B2

SO-ADX-295

DATE DUE

Emma S. Johnson

Study in Hosea

Books by the Author

DIGEST OF THE DIVINE LAW
STUDY IN REVELATION
STUDY IN DANIEL
STUDY IN JEREMIAH
PRIMOGENESIS
BEHOLD, HE COMETH!
DOCUMENTARY STUDIES, VOLUME I
DOCUMENTARY STUDIES, VOLUME II
DOCUMENTARY STUDIES, VOLUME III

STUDY
IN HOSEA

by Howard B. Rand, LL.B.

UNITY SCHOOL LIBRARY
Unity Village
Lee's Summit, Missouri 64063

DESTINY PUBLISHERS
Haverhill, Massachusetts

Copyright 1955 in U. S. A.

By Destiny Publishers
Haverhill, Mass.

All rights reserved
Including the right to reproduce this book or
portions thereof in any form

Library of Congress Catalog Card Number: 55-12181

PRINTED IN THE UNITED STATES OF AMERICA

INTRODUCTION

WHILE HOSEA IS NUMBERED among the minor prophets because of the shortness of his book, its message is by no means secondary in importance. In graphic, sometimes symbolic, terms Hosea tells the story of the rejection, the punishment, the regathering and the ultimate restoration of the House of Israel. In one bold sweep across the centuries, beginning with the dispersion of the House of Israel and climaxing in their redemption, the resurrection of their rulers and the restoration of the Kingdom, followed by universal peace and prosperity, the prophet provides a telescopic preview of the march of the House of Israel down through the pages of history.

This prophet clearly sets forth the distinction between Israel and Judah and justifies God's dealings with His people in judgment. If any doubt remains concerning the division of the people of the Kingdom into two separate entities—the House of Israel and the House of Judah—and the identification of the Anglo-Saxon-Celtic peoples with the House of Israel today, a careful study of Hosea's prophecies should settle the question beyond refutation. The prophet provides a more comprehensive understanding of why God allowed Israel to be carried captive into Assyria than may be found anywhere else in the Scriptures.

The northern ten-tribed Kingdom of Israel is depicted symbolically as an unfaithful wife whom God divorced and sent away into Assyrian bondage. Hosea had warned the people of impending judgment for their sins, making it clear to them that they would not escape punishment if they persisted in transgressing the commandments, statutes and judgments of the Lord and partaking of the idolatrous practices of the nations around them. Yet, in the midst of condemning the people for their evil ways, Hosea looked forward in vision to behold the coming glorious deliverance when the unfaithful wife would be forgiven and the bill of divorcement would be blotted out.

Marking the downward steps in the great apostasy in Israel, and seeing the glory of the Lord leave His people, Hosea used another and more spectacular analogy to forecast the years of bitter tribulation which the House of Israel would be compelled to endure. He predicted their national demise in terms of the "burial" of the House of Israel in the "graveyard" of Assyrian captivity. Nevertheless, under the inspiration of the Holy Spirit, the prophet looked forward to the day when they would be ransomed from the grave and live again in God's sight.

This, the prophet makes plain, will be the outcome of the sacrificial work of Jesus Christ, the Redeemer of Israel. Their ultimate restoration is therefore assured and this will come to pass when the Anglo-Saxon-Celtic peoples awaken to a recognition of their origin and identity as the House of Israel in the world today.

This book has been written in the hope that it will assist the reader in a deeper comprehension of the writings of the Prophet Hosea.

THE AUTHOR

September 16, 1955
Haverhill, Massachusetts

CONTENTS

CHAPTER   PAGE

Introduction   v

I. Day of Jezreel   1

II. Bill of Divorcement   16

III. The Acceptable Time   31

IV. A Promised Deliverance   48

V. Impending Judgment   59

VI. A Great Apostasy   77

VII. Transgressing the Covenant   93

VIII. The Departing Glory   109

IX. Ransomed From the Grave   125

X. Life From the Dead   135

Index   149

CHAPTER I
Day of Jezreel

THE MINOR PROPHETS are so named, not because their utterances were less inspired than those of the rest of the prophets, but because their prophecies were shorter than those of the group called the major prophets (Isaiah, Jeremiah, Ezekiel, Daniel). There are twelve minor prophets and Hosea's book is given first place in this section of the Scriptures. Six of the writings of these prophets are dated and six are not. Hosea's book is one that is dated, for we are told that he prophesied during the reigns of Uzziah, Jotham, Ahaz and Hezekiah, Kings of Judah, and in the days of Jeroboam, the son of Joash, King of Israel (Hosea 1: 1). Adding together the length of the reigns of the kings of Judah, and the fact that Hosea was active up to the time of the fall of Samaria, capital city of the northern ten-tribed Kingdom of Israel, this prophet was engaged in his work for from seventy to seventy-five years.

Contemporary prophets who were active during the time Hosea was prophesying were Isaiah, Joel, Amos and Jonah. It is very likely that, as a young man, Hosea had been a member of the school of the prophets founded by

Elijah, which was carried on by Elisha after the ascension of Elijah.

PROPHET'S COMMISSION

The true spelling of the prophet's name, taken from the Hebrew, is Hoshea, which means *"salvation."* Nothing is known about Hosea, his family or his personal history other than what is recorded in his book. We do know he was a prophet to the northern ten-tribed Kingdom of Israel (the House of Israel), although he directed some messages to Judah also. The burden of Hosea's prophecy had to do with the coming end of the northern ten-tribed Kingdom and the deportation of the House of Israel. He was specifically instructed to go and take a wife as follows:

> "Go, take unto thee a wife of whoredoms, and children of whoredoms: for the land hath committed great whoredom, departing from the Lord." (Hosea 1: 2.)

Many consider the Lord's instructions to Hosea very strange indeed, but the manner of his marriage and family life were as much a part of the Lord's commission to the prophet as the Lord's instructions to Jeremiah to wear a heavy yoke on one occasion and His command to Ezekiel to lie on his side for a number of days for the iniquity of the House of Israel and for the iniquity of the House of Judah. These were demonstrations of an unusual nature, the symbolic meaning of which could not fail to be understood. Equally so, the Lord called upon Hosea to enact a role in his own life that was a dramatization of the Lord's relationship with His people. The future recital of Hosea's personal experiences was to bring home to the House of Israel the enormity of their sins and serve as evidence in justification of the action taken by the Lord in punishing His people.

CRITIC'S CONTENTION

There has been a great deal of conjecture about the directions to Hosea to take "a wife of whoredoms." Actually Hosea was being told to take a wife from among the women of the Northern Kingdom of Israel, for they had all turned to idolatry after departing from the commandments, statutes and judgments of the Lord. When Hosea married a woman of the House of Israel, it was regarded as taking an idolatress to become his wife. This wife, the mother of his children, symbolically represented the House of Israel, for when Israel turned to idolatry, the Northern Kingdom was likened to an unfaithful wife. The House of Israel had apostatized to the extent that the time was drawing near when God was to write a bill of divorcement and send them away because of their unfaithfulness to Him who was "an husband unto them."

Some critics have contended that Hosea did not actually marry such a woman and in order to escape the plain facts as written concerning the instructions God gave to Hosea, they construe the entire matter as allegorical. One critic even declares:

> "It is a scandal to think of Hosea being commanded to take an unchaste wife and without any reluctance obeying such a command."

But why should the critic question God and His purposes? Hosea was being used to demonstrate, through his own experiences, what the Lord was enduring at the hands of His people Israel. It is certain that the prophet did marry one who had been brought up in idolatry, since this was true of the majority of families in the Northern Kingdom. It is also true that idolatry, as practiced in those days, bred faithlessness to marriage ties because of its licentiousness and moral degradation.

HOSEA'S MARRIAGE

Hosea was obedient to the Divine instructions:

"So he went and took Gomer the daughter of Diblaim." (Hosea 1: 3.)

It is interesting to note that the meaning of the name "Gomer," the prophet's wife, is *"consuming,"* while that of Diblaim, her father, means *"withered"*—words graphically descriptive of the results following the immorality and degeneration prevalent in the land of Israel at that time due to the great apostasy.

It has never been definitely ascertained whether Hosea resided in the territory belonging to the House of Israel or that of Judah, for his book does not specifically settle this question. However, the fact that he acknowledged the House of David, naming the kings occupying the throne in Jerusalem during the time of his prophetic work, could have been the result of his loyalty to that House because he resided in the territory of the Southern Kingdom. By mentioning the King of Israel—Jeroboam, the son of Joash—the prophet would be designating the ruler of the House of Israel at the time his messages were first directed against the Northern Kingdom. It was not uncommon for a prophet to be residing in one kingdom and be instructed by the Lord to become a prophet to the other kingdom. In fact, the history of those times indicates that most of the men commissioned by God to prophesy to the Northern Kingdom did come out of Judah, for the apostasy was so great in Israel that only false prophets flourished in the land (I Kings 13: 1-10).

The command to "go" and the fact that Hosea "went" to the Northern Kingdom of Israel to secure a wife could be construed to mean that he made a journey from the land of Judah to that of Israel in order to fulfill the word of the Lord that had come to him. Such a journey as this to secure a wife under all the circumstances that would enter into the marriage could very well have contributed to bringing his mission to the attention of the people of the House of Israel and to their king.

MEANING OF NAMES

Many times in the history of God's people men were named to commemorate outstanding happenings. After Abel was slain, Eve named her next son Seth, which means *"appointed,"* for she knew he was the progenitor of the appointed seed (*i.e.,* the chosen people). One of the sons of Eber (Heber) was Peleg, which means *"division,"* "for in his days was the earth divided [by seismic disturbances]" (Gen. 10: 25). When the Ark of the Covenant was taken by the Philistines in battle, Samuel's daughter-in-law gave birth to a son whom she named Ichabod, which means *"inglorious,"* for she said, "The glory is departed from Israel: for the ark of God is taken" (I Sam. 4: 22).

HOSEA'S FIRST CHILD

Gomer bore Hosea a son and the Lord instructed the prophet to call him Jezreel, a name that has two meanings: *"may God scatter"* and *"may God sow":*

5

"For yet a little while, and I will avenge [visit] the blood of Jezreel upon the house of Jehu, and will cause to cease the kingdom of the house of Israel." (Hosea 1: 4.)

It was in the valley of Jezreel that Jehu killed both the King of Israel and the King of Judah, and it was there also where he drove his chariot over the body of Jezebel. While Jehu carried out the judgment previously pronounced by God upon the house of Ahab, he did so to make himself secure in his own rise to power rather than as a service rendered the Lord. The following footnote in *The Companion Bible* is of interest here:

"Jehu had carried out the judgment of God on the house of Ahab because it accorded with his own will; but he was guilty of murder because it was not executed purely according to the will of God. He would have disobeyed if it had not served his own interest. This is seen from the fact that he practiced Jeroboam's idolatries, for which Ahab had been judged."

Because Jehu had brought judgment upon the house of Ahab, God told him:

"Thy children of the fourth generation shall sit on the throne of Israel." (II Kings 10: 30.)

Jeroboam, son of Joash, was the third generation, in whose reign Hosea prophesied. The "little while" in the prophecy accompanying the naming of Hosea's son referred to the fact that one more generation of Jehu's descendants would come to the throne, after which God would be free to move to avenge the blood of Jezreel upon the house of Jehu, with subsequent judgments bringing to an end the kingdom of the House of Israel.

However, the deeper significance of the name Jezreel (*God sows*) was prophetic of judgment combined with mercy for, when the purpose of the judgment upon the House of Israel was accomplished, there was to be a future deliverance. The scattering and sowing in judgment was later to be a regathering and resowing in mercy. Ferrar Fenton renders this verse:

"Then the Ever-living said to him, 'Call his name Jezreel, —for before long I will fix the murders of Jezreel upon the House of Jehu, and abolish the kingship of Israel; and at the same time I will break the bow of Israel in the valley of God's Harvest.' "

THE SECOND CHILD

Gomer then conceived and bore a daughter and God commanded the prophet to name her Lo-ruhamah:

"For I will no more have mercy upon the house of Israel; but I will utterly take them away." (Hosea 1: 6.)

Lo-ruhamah means *"not compassionated"* and is rendered in Romans 9: 25 as "not beloved." Peter, referring to the casting away of Israel, renders the meaning of this name, "not having obtained mercy" (I Peter 2: 10).

SPECIFIC DISTINCTIONS

Following this pronouncement upon the House of Israel that they were no longer to obtain mercy, the Lord, through Hosea, reassured the House of Judah:

"But I will have mercy upon the house of Judah, and will save them by the Lord their God." (Hosea 1: 7.)

This statement shows very clearly the contrast between the retribution that the House of Israel was about to receive for their idolatrous practices and the protection the House of Judah would have when the armies of the Gentiles encamped against Samaria. When Samaria was captured and Israel was carried away into Assyrian captivity, Jerusalem escaped a similar fate at that time. It was not saved by sword or by battle, as the prophet declared, but rather by the Lord who protected Judah from the ravages of war.

This contrast between Judah and Israel is, in itself, sufficient evidence to demonstrate that they represent two separate and distinct peoples, with God dealing in a different way with each. It is not the Word of the Lord, nor the statements of His prophets, nor the records of Scriptural history, which confuse the issue by failing to distinguish between the two sections of God's people, their past, their present and their future. Rather, it is modern scholarship and many theologians who are responsible for so much misunderstanding concerning these clearly-defined differences and the respective peoples who today represent the modern House of Israel as separate and distinct from the descendants of the House of Judah.

THE THIRD CHILD

When Gomer had weaned Lo-ruhamah, she conceived and gave birth to a son:

"Then said God, Call his name Lo-ammi; for ye are not my people, and I will not be your God." (Hosea 1: 9.)

This was the climax of the sequence of prophecies based upon the naming of the three children of Hosea and Gomer. Now the people were wholly repudiated, for their cup of iniquity was full. Yet this prophecy was no sooner voiced than another prophecy was given that would be difficult indeed to fathom if we did not have the fulfillment of it before our very eyes in these latter days.

SONS OF GOD

Immediately following the pronouncement that the House of Israel would not be God's people and that He would not be their God, the Lord declared through Hosea:

> "Yet the number of the children of Israel shall be as the sand of the sea, which cannot be measured nor numbered; and it shall come to pass, that in the place where it was said unto them, Ye are not my people, there it shall be said unto them, Ye are the sons of the living God." (Hosea 1: 10.)

This was a look into the future, to a time far removed from the days of the Prophet Hosea, when, in conformity with the covenant promise made to Abraham, Isaac and Jacob, their descendants would become a great multitude. At that time the nations of modern Israel would be residing in a new location and would be ignorant of their identity as the seed of Abraham. Yet, in the very place where men would be saying they are not God's people Israel, it would be said of them that they are the sons of the living God. This can refer to nothing less than the fact that the term "Christian" (which means sons of God through Jesus Christ) would be applied to those among them who seek the Lord their Saviour. It could only apply to the time when the House of Israel would be Christianized and under the New Covenant, seeking Him whom they rejected by refusing to keep the terms of the Old Covenant.

A CHRISTIAN PEOPLE

Moses declared that Israel would in the latter days be identified as Christian by conformity with the require-

ments of circumcision according to the Christian standard:

> "And the Lord thy God will circumcise thine heart, and
> the heart of thy seed, to love the Lord thy God with all
> thine heart, and with all thy soul, that thou mayest live."
> (Deut. 30: 6.)

This type of circumcision did not come into being until
after the Church was born at Pentecost, after which
Christian circumcision was stated by Paul to be as follows:

> "Circumcision is that of the heart, in the spirit, and not
> in the letter." (Rom. 2: 29.)

That the House of Israel was to find grace following
their deportation is clear from Jeremiah's prophecy:

> "Thus saith the Lord, The people which were left of
> the sword found grace in the wilderness; even Israel, when
> I went to cause him to rest." (Jer. 31: 2.)

This was to be after their escape westward from Assyrian captivity, when they had come to rest in the "appointed place." It is quite significant that Isaiah the
Prophet addressed a special message to a Christianized
people who are wholly unaware of their origin and that
Abraham was their father and Sarah their mother. This
prophet's exhortation is for them to awaken to the knowledge of these facts:

> "Hearken to me, ye that follow after righteousness, ye that
> seek the Lord: look unto the rock whence ye are hewn, and
> to the hole of the pit whence ye are digged. Look unto
> Abraham your father, and unto Sarah that bare you." (Isa.
> 51: 1-2.)

Smith and Goodspeed render this:

> "Listen to me, you who press after deliverance, you who
> seek the Lord! Look to the rock from which you were hewn,

and the quarry from which you were dug; look to Abraham your father, and to Sarah who bore you!"

Under no conditions do the Jews fulfill these requirements, for they acknowledge their origin but do not recognize or accept salvation through Jesus Christ, the Messiah. However, the Anglo-Saxon-Celtic peoples, as Christians, in their songs and in their church services, continually proclaim that they are the sons of the living God, while at the same time church leaders and laymen together vehemently deny that they are the descendants of Abraham, Isaac and Jacob!

APPOINT ONE HEAD

The final outcome of this particular message given through Hosea follows:

> "Then shall the children of Judah and the children of Israel be gathered together, and appoint themselves one head, and they shall come up out of the land: for great shall be the day of Jezreel." (Hosea 1: 11.)

Appoint themselves one head! Jeremiah refers to the "shepherds" who have scattered the sheep of His pasture, and against these false pastors God pronounces judgment for their evil works. It is at that time that the "one head" is to be appointed. Although His people have become Christianized, yet, under the leadership of modernist "shepherds," they are in danger of being destroyed, so the Lord condemns the shepherds who have refused to feed His flock:

> "Ye have scattered my flock, and driven them away, and have not visited them: behold, I will visit upon you the evil of your doings, saith the Lord. And I will gather the remnant of my flock out of all countries whither I have driven them, and will bring them again to their folds; and

they shall be fruitful and increase. And I will set up shepherds over them which shall feed them; and they shall fear no more, nor be dismayed, neither shall they be lacking, saith the Lord. Behold, the days come, saith the Lord, that I will raise unto David a righteous Branch, and a King shall reign and prosper, and shall execute judgment and justice in the earth. In his days Judah shall be saved, and Israel shall dwell safely: and this is his name whereby he shall be called, The Lord our Righteousness." (Jer. 23: 2-6.)

It is Jesus Christ, who is the Lord our Righteousness, who will become the appointed Head. Ezekiel confirms this, for after also condemning the false leadership that has caused His people to go astray, the Lord declares through that prophet:

"Therefore will I save my flock, and they shall no more be a prey; and I will judge between cattle and cattle. And I will set up one shepherd over them, and he shall feed them, even my servant David; he shall feed them, and he shall be their shepherd." (Ez. 34: 22-23.)

Ferrar Fenton renders this:

"I will protect My sheep, and they shall not again become a prey, for I will decide between sheep and sheep, and will appoint a Perfect Shepherd, who will shepherd them,—My Servant David,—who shall pasture them, and be their shepherd."

JESUS CHRIST, MASTER SHEPHERD

Our Lord Jesus Christ is the only one who can qualify as the Perfect Shepherd and He definitely associates Himself with the Shepherd's office:

"I am the good shepherd, and know my sheep, and am known of mine. As the Father knoweth me, even so know

I the Father: and I lay down my life for the sheep." (John
10: 14-15.)

In *Study in Daniel** (pp. 344-359), the subject of the
Ancient Order of Master Shepherds is dealt with in full
and it is pointed out that "Jesus Christ, the Grand Master
of all Master Shepherds, wore the insignia of his office as
Shepherd of the flock." Then the question is asked:

> "Who are His sheep for whom He was willing to lay
> down His life? They are none other than Israel. He came
> that they might be redeemed. When He commissioned His
> disciples to preach the Gospel of the Kingdom, He sent
> them to the sheep of His pasture, saying:
> " 'Go not into the way of the Gentiles, and into any city
> of the Samaritans enter ye not: But go rather to the lost
> sheep of the house of Israel. And as ye go, preach, saying,
> The Kingdom of heaven is at hand.' (Matt. 10: 5-7.)"

DAY OF JUDGMENT

Hosea speaks of the "day of Jezreel" as the time when
all this will come to pass. This became a prophetic term
indicative of a day of judgment by cleansing, for the original site of Jezreel, a fruitful field, had been defiled with
blood. Our Lord Himself speaks of the age ending in
judgment and, as a result of its severity, the House of
Israel and the House of Judah will turn to the Lord.

While the King James Version renders Hosea 1: 11 as
"they shall come up out of the land: for great shall be
the day of Jezreel," it is quite significant to note Ferrar
Fenton's translation direct from the Hebrew:

> "For I will collect the children of Judah, and the chil-
> dren of Israel together, and they will appoint a Single

* $5.00 postpaid. Destiny Publishers, Haverhill, Mass.

Head for themselves and rise up from the earth for the Great Day of God's Harvest."

The Great Day of God's Harvest is the time of the resurrection when He shall send forth His angels to gather out of His Kingdom all who offend and do iniquity (Matt. 13: 41). The Great Day of Jezreel, or the Great Day of God's Harvest, to which Hosea refers, which is also the Great and Terrible Day of the Lord spoken of by Joel "as a time of trouble such as never was since there was a nation," is the time of judgment, to the end of which Daniel refers by stating:

"And many of them that sleep in the dust of the earth shall awake." (Dan. 12: 2.)

Ferrar Fenton's rendering of Hosea 1: 11 bears this out, for he indicates there is to be a literal *rising up from the earth* in the Great Day of God's Harvest! It was of that harvest time that Isaiah was prophesying when he exclaimed:

"Awake and sing, ye that dwell in dust: for thy dew is as the dew of herbs." (Isa. 26: 19.)

The inference to be drawn from Hosea's statement is far-reaching indeed, showing that Hosea's grasp of the whole sweep of prophecy was no less complete than that of the major prophets. The prophet's reference to the fact that Judah and Israel will appoint themselves one head in that day is evidently indicative of the wholehearted acceptance of Jesus Christ that will ensue as the result of the pressure of judgment that will compel a turning to Him for deliverance. Here is a wonderfully clear glimpse of the future when, just preceding the time of restoration, both Judah and Israel will become willing subjects of the coming King. All Israel at that time, both the living and the resurrected, will acknowledge Him as their Saviour and Redeemer. Then He will come and take the throne of His father David, for the people will be willing in the day of His power to accept Him as their King so that He may rule over them.

CHAPTER II

Bill of Divorcement

JEZEBEL, the wife of Ahab, had introduced Baal worship in Israel, having brought it from her native land, for she was a daughter of Ethbaal, King of the Zidonians. During the reign of Ahab, Elijah had placed before the people a choice as to whether they would serve Baal or worship Jehovah their God. But in spite of the demonstration that the Lord is God, acknowledged by the exclamation uttered by those who witnessed the descent of the fire of God upon Elijah's altar (I Kings 18: 39), Baalism was not rejected. As time passed the people, by their actions rather than by their words, chose to serve Baal. Because this was the situation throughout the Northern Kingdom of the House of Israel in the days of Hosea, the Lord sent this prophet to witness against them.

The daughters of Israel had become temple women, consecrated to a licentious worship associated with the most degrading practices, which became mandatory as a religious duty. As a result adultery became widespread throughout the land. The festivals of the former residents of Canaan were observed in every detail by Israel, causing Hosea to declare that the people had completely turned

16

their backs upon the Lord their God, dishonoring Him and breaking their covenant with Him.

THE PEOPLE REPUDIATED

It was because of these conditions that God had instructed Hosea to marry a wife taken from among the women of the Northern Kingdom, to whom children had been born. The names given these children at the time of their birth signified God's attitude toward Israel and the conditions extant throughout the entire land. In the name of the prophet's daughter, Lo-ruhamah; that is, "not having obtained mercy," and his son, Lo-ammi; that is, "not my people," God set forth what would be the ultimate result of Israel's persistence in following the practices of Baalism and worshipping idols.

A FAITHFUL REMNANT

The symbolism was somewhat changed in the next message given by the Lord and the second chapter of Hosea's book opens with the statement:

> "Say ye unto your brethren, Ammi; and to your sisters, Ruhamah. Plead with your mother, plead: for she is not my wife, neither am I her husband." (Hosea 2: 1-2.)

Ammi means "my people" and Ruhamah means "having obtained mercy." Because the prophet was instructed to drop the prefix "Lo" in each case in addressing Israel, it indicates that in this instance Hosea was directing his message to a certain group among the people. There were some individuals and a number of families in the Northern Kingdom who had not succumbed to idolatry and Baalism. It was these to whom the prophet was speaking.

By this application of the symbolism we are reminded of the fact that when Elijah felt that he alone was left of all in Israel who had acknowledged God, the Lord informed him:

> "I have left me seven thousand in Israel, all the knees which have not bowed unto Baal, and every mouth which hath not kissed him." (I Kings 19: 18.)

While this group was very small in comparison to the whole population, yet it was a sufficient number to witness to those who had turned away from the Lord, pointing out that their ways were evil. It is very evident that in the time of Hosea there was such a remnant among the House of Israel who had remained true to their God. It was to this small core of faithful men and women that the prophet was directed to speak.

He asked them to plead with their "mother," the House of Israel, a designation referring to the governmental authority of the nation. They were directed to declare to her that, because of her unfaithfulness, God was disclaiming her as His wife, repudiating His former relationship:

> "For thy Maker is thine husband; the Lord of hosts is his name." (Isa. 54: 5.)

They were to intensify their work of witnessing since the time was at hand when the Northern Kingdom was to be carried away into Assyria unless they repented and turned to the Lord. These faithful few were instructed to plead with the nation, calling upon the people to turn from their idolatry and stop embracing Baalism. To persist in their evil ways was to bring upon themselves the five aspects of judgment given in symbolic terms:

"Lest I strip her naked, and set her as in the day that she was born, and make her as a wilderness, and set her like a dry land, and slay her with thirst." (Hosea 2: 3.)

THE LAND MADE DESOLATE

Here we have the prophet referring to the coming desolation of the land if the people refused to heed the call to repentance. Furthermore, if the House of Israel failed to hearken and turn away from Baalism, their children of succeeding generations would also suffer:

"And upon her children I will have no pity, Because they are harlot's children. For their mother played the harlot; She who bore them acted shamelessly. For she said, 'I will go after my lovers, who give me my bread and my water, my wool and my flax, my oil and my drink.' " (Hosea 2: 4-5, *Smith & Goodspeed Trans.*)

Her lovers were her Baals, or lords, from whom Israel was claiming she received the necessities of life such as food, drink and clothing, as well as the luxuries that contributed to her happiness. This recognition of Baal was given in the celebration of the festivals in honor of the deity, during the rites of which Baal was acknowledged as the giver of all material prosperity. The Lord held this as tantamount to a wife bestowing her affections on another. The homage rendered to Baal for such gifts is also likened to the hire of an abandoned woman.

THE REJECTED WIFE

Having wholeheartedly accepted the idolatrous worship of Baalism, the House of Israel refused to heed the plea of Hosea and of the faithful few among them who had not bowed their knees before the heathen god. Therefore, the House of Israel became "not my people"—a designation foretold by the prophet—and the instructions to Ammi and Ruhamah to say to their mother, "she is not my wife," became a reality. Because of Israel's failure to cease all idolatrous practices and serve the Lord only, God wrote them a bill of divorcement and put them away. From that time forward Israel (not Judah) was under the curse of the law which Moses had recorded as a part of the Law of the Lord in these words:

> "When a man hath taken a wife, and married her, and it come to pass that she find no favour in his eyes, because he hath found some uncleanness [indecency] in her: then let him write her a bill of divorcement, and give it in her hand, and send her out of his house. And when she is departed out of his house, she may go and be another man's wife. And if the latter husband hate her, and write her a bill of divorcement, and giveth it in her hand, and sendeth her out of his house; or if the latter husband die, which took her to be his wife; her former husband, which sent her away, may not take her again to be his wife, after that she is defiled; for that is abomination before the Lord." (Deut. 24: 1-4.)

In conformity with the requirements of this law, God placed in Israel's hand the bill of divorcement. Through His prophets God had warned her that this was what He would do if she failed to amend her ways. Israel refused, so Jeremiah records the fact that such a bill of divorcement was given to the Northern Kingdom, or House of Israel.

JUDAH NOT DIVORCED

Following this a very interesting observation was made by Jeremiah:

"And I saw, when for all the causes whereby backsliding Israel committed adultery I had put her away, and given her a bill of divorce; yet her treacherous sister Judah feared not, but went and played the harlot [*i.e.*, embraced idolatry] also." (Jer. 3: 8.)

This is a clear statement of the fact that Israel was divorced, *but Judah was not divorced*. Yet, in spite of this strong evidence of the distinction between the House of Israel and the House of Judah, the teachings of the majority of theologians undertake to declare Israel and Judah to be one and the same people. The error of holding such a position becomes more and more apparent as one analyzes God's dealings with the House of Israel, which were altogether different from His dealings with the House of Judah.

Could Not Return

The House of Israel was sent away into Assyrian captivity and about 130 years later Judah was carried away to Babylon. Because Israel had been given a bill of divorcement, and Judah had not, Israel was unable to return to Palestine, while a remnant of the House of Judah did return after the Divinely-set term of the Babylonian captivity had expired. According to the law, when God gave the House of Israel a bill of divorcement, He sent her away out of the "promised land." So long as that bill of divorcement was in force, He could not take her back into His house, *i.e.*, into His land, to dwell again.

A Future Return

However, that there is to be a return to the land in the future is a very clearly stated fact of Scripture—and it is

Israel who is to return to the land of their fathers in the sense that they will regain possession and control of the territory. Ezekiel declares:

> "Thus saith the Lord God; in the day that I shall have cleansed you from all your iniquities I will also cause you to dwell in the cities, and the wastes shall be builded. And the desolate land shall be tilled. . . . As the holy flock, as the flock of Jerusalem in her solemn feasts; so shall the waste cities be filled with flocks of men: and they shall know that I am the Lord." (Ez. 36: 33-38.)

But before this can come to pass, the bill of divorcement given to Israel must be annulled. Paul declared that only the death of the husband could bring freedom from the curse of this law:

> "Know ye not, brethren, (for I speak to them that know the law) how that the law hath dominion over a man as long as he liveth? For the woman which hath an husband is bound by the law to her husband so long as he liveth; but if the husband be dead, she is loosed from the law of her husband." (Rom. 7: 1-2.)

Therefore, the only way that the House of Israel could escape the penalty of the law would be through the death of Him who had given her the bill of divorcement. This is the reason Jesus Christ, God the Son, who gave His life on Calvary's cross, is called the Redeemer, for He redeemed His people Israel from the curse of this law. In anticipation of His death and resurrection, Jesus commissioned His disciples to "go unto the lost sheep of the House of Israel" and proclaim the good news of their redemption.

Upon their acceptance of the fact of their redemption, they would be in a position to be restored to that which had been lost to them. Eventually they would be permitted to return to the land that was previously theirs, for it is to Israel, Christianized and sincerely repentant, that Zephaniah's message is addressed:

"The remnant of Israel shall not do iniquity, nor speak lies; neither shall a deceitful tongue be found in their mouth. . . . The Lord hath taken away thy judgments, he hath cast out thine enemy: the king of Israel, even the Lord, is in the midst of thee: thou shalt not see evil any more. . . . At that time will I bring you again, even in the time that I gather you: for I will make you a name and a praise among all people of the earth, when I turn back your captivity before your eyes, saith the Lord." (Zeph. 3: 13-20.)

But let it be noted that it is only as a Christian people that Israel may regain possession of their land. These simple facts of jurisprudence should forever settle all questions concerning the return of Israel to Palestine.

THE WESTWARD TREK

After their escape from Assyrian captivity, the people of the House of Israel, being barred from returning to their land again, moved westward from the land of their captors —a fact which can be amply verified by painstaking research in the records of history.* Because of the seemingly hopeless situation in which the people found themselves as a result of having been given a bill of divorcement, the Lord, through Ezekiel, represents them as dry bones filling a valley, symbolizing a people who were in complete despair:

"Then he said unto me, Son of man, these bones are the

---

* See *Chemivision* by William J. Hale, Chapters I to X, for details of the westward trek of Israel and the names under which the different tribes moved across southern and central Europe. $3.00 postpaid, Destiny Publishers, Haverhill, Mass.

whole house of Israel: behold, they say, Our bones are dried, and our hope is lost: we are cut off for our parts." (Ez. 37: 11.)

Smith and Goodspeed translate this passage as follows:

"Then he said to me, O mortal man, these bones are the whole house of Israel. Behold, they keep saying, Our bones are dried up, and our hope is lost; we are completely cut off."

This applies to the House of Israel, not Judah. Through Ezekiel the Lord shows with what abandonment the House of Israel had turned to idolatry:

"Thus saith the Lord God; Are ye polluted after the manner of your fathers? And commit ye whoredom after their abominations? For when ye offer your gifts, when ye make your sons to pass through the fire, ye pollute yourselves with all your idols, even unto this day: and shall I be enquired of by you, O house of Israel? As I live, saith the Lord God, I will not be enquired of by you." (Ez. 20: 30-31.)

Bond of the Covenant

Evidently as a result of the Lord's rejection of Israel, the people decided that they would become like the heathen and forget their covenant with their God. In this way they expected to secure for themselves a position at least equal to that occupied by the heathen who enjoyed a certain type of prosperity. But knowing their thoughts and desires, the Lord declared:

"And that which cometh into your mind shall not be at all, that ye say, We will be as the heathen, as the families of the countries, to serve wood and stone." (Ez. 20: 32.)

Even though the Lord had divorced the House of Israel, they were not free from the terms of His everlasting covenant with them. His intention was to compel them to come under its terms by the operation of the "But" clauses of the covenant which set forth the penalties for its violation. Incidentally, the very fact that the House of Israel was to suffer in accordance with the penalties set forth in the covenant clearly demonstrates that the covenant was not set aside. Confirming this position, the Lord declares:

"As I live, saith the Lord God, surely with a mighty hand, and with a stretched out arm, and with fury poured out, will I rule over you: And I will bring you out from the people, and will gather you out of the countries wherein ye are scattered, with a mighty hand, and with a stretched out arm, and with fury poured out. And I will bring you into the wilderness of the people, and there will I plead with you face to face. Like as I pleaded with your fathers in the wilderness of the land of Egypt, so will I plead with you, saith the Lord God. And I will cause you to pass under the rod, and I will bring you into the bond of the covenant." (Ez. 20: 33-37.)

ROD OF PUNISHMENT

Hosea foretold the beginning of this pressure that God proposed to exert upon the House of Israel and he corroborated Ezekiel's prediction when he recorded what the Lord had said:

"Therefore, behold, I will hedge up thy way with thorns, and make a wall, that she shall not find her paths. And she shall follow after her lovers, but she shall not overtake them; and she shall seek them, but shall not find them: then shall she say, I will go and return to my first husband; for then was it better with me than now." (Hosea 2: 6-7.)

The first results of the rod of punishment upon the House of Israel for their apostasy was the destruction of their prosperity. The misery and perplexities that followed soon brought home to them the futility of trying to secure the necessities and luxuries of life by serving Baal. Then they decided it was better to serve the Lord rather than Baal. This was not because of any great spiritual awakening, but with the idea that they would pay homage to Him as they had paid homage to Baal, expecting by so doing to secure the rewards of fruitfulness and prosperity with which they had formerly been blessed. Actually the desire was but to exchange one god for another simply in the hope of securing material prosperity. However, the Lord who is God is not interested in such reasons for serving Him—a type of service that at best would be outward only. Instead of accepting this shallow homage, the Lord declared openly that Israel did not know He had all the while given them the corn and wine, with the oil and the wealth of silver and gold, which they had used to honor Baal:

"Therefore will I return, and take away my corn in the time thereof, and my wine in the season thereof, and will recover my wool and my flax given to cover her nakedness. And now will I discover her lewdness [expose her shame] in the sight of her lovers, and none shall deliver her out of mine hand." (Hosea 2: 9-10.)

By taking away all her prosperity, God reduced the House of Israel to a state of poverty. He refused to continue to allow them to have the blessings of prosperity on the basis of lip service, with its ritualistic forms and ceremonies. Even the heathen and their gods would not acknowledge Israel because God's hand rested heavily in judgment upon her. The Lord declared:

"I will also cause all her mirth to cease, her feast days, her new moons, and her sabbaths, and all her solemn feasts.

And I will destroy her vines and her fig trees, whereof she hath said, These are my rewards that my lovers have given me: and I will make them a forest, and the beasts of the field shall eat them." (Hosea 2: 11-12.)

In this way Hosea succinctly describes the coming desolation of the land as a result of the deportation of the House of Israel, which was about to be carried away into Assyrian captivity. The prophet then pronounced judgment upon the people for having turned to idolatry, burning incense to heathen gods and attributing their prosperity to Baal:

"And I will visit upon her the days of Baalim, wherein she burned incense to them, and she decked herself with her earrings and her jewels, and she went after her lovers, and forgat me, saith the Lord." (Hosea 2: 13.)

Days of Baalim

What is meant by visiting upon Israel the days of Baalim? The period from the time of the Exodus in 1486 B.C. to the great deportation in 721 B.C. comprises 765 years. The history of God's people during those years was one of vacillation between serving God and Baal. During the period of the Judges, and also in the reign of the kings, idolatry often flourished in the land and homage was paid to Baal. However, the land was practically free from such idolatry during the reign of David and it was not until Solomon was led astray by his wives that idolatry was established in the land again.

When the House of Israel revolted from the rule of Rehoboam, Solomon's son, idolatry was already on the increase among the people of the Northern Kingdom. It is safe to say, therefore, that during at least half of the 765 years from the time of the Exodus to the capture of

Samaria, and the deportation of the House of Israel to Assyria in 721 B.C., idolatry flourished in the land. The mention of visiting the "days of Baalim" upon Israel, and the subsequent period of punishment, would lead to the assumption that 360 years of the 765 years were marred by idolatrous practices in the land. With the rounding out of the number of years that constitute a *time*—360 years —the cup of Israel's iniquity was now full. The judgment that was to be visited upon them under the law was to be according to the days they served Baal multiplied by seven—Seven Times, *i.e.*, 2520 years.

> "And if ye will not for all this hearken unto me, but walk contrary unto me; Then I will walk contrary unto you also in fury; and I, even I, will chastise you seven times for your sins." (Lev. 26: 27-28.)

It is interesting to note that a namesake of the prophet came to the throne of Israel (the prophet's name in Hebrew being Hoshea) and, in the ninth year of the reign of King Hoshea, the king of Assyria took Samaria and carried Israel away into the land of Assyria, placing them in Halah and in Habor by the river of Gozan, and in the cities of the Medes. This was the beginning of the Great Captivity and of the Seven Times of punishment for their national sins. The reason given for the deportation is set forth in the Book of II Kings:

> "For so it was that the children of Israel had sinned against the Lord their God, which had brought them up out of the land of Egypt, from under the hand of Pharaoh king of Egypt, and had feared other gods, and walked in the statutes of the heathen, whom the Lord cast out from before the children of Israel, and of the kings of Israel, which they had made. And the children of Israel did secretly those things that were not right against the Lord

their God, and they built them high places in all their cities, from the tower of the watchmen to the fenced city. And they set them up images and groves in every high hill, and under every green tree: And there they burnt incense in all the high places, as did the heathen whom the Lord carried away before them; and wrought wicked things to provoke the Lord to anger: For they served idols, whereof the Lord had said unto them, Ye shall not do this thing. Yet the Lord testified against Israel, and against Judah, by all the prophets, and by all the seers, saying, Turn ye from your evil ways, and keep my commandments and my statutes, according to all the law which I commanded your fathers, and which I sent to you by my servants the prophets. Notwithstanding they would not hear, but hardened their necks, like to the neck of their fathers, that did not believe in the Lord their God. And they rejected his statutes, and his covenant that he made with their fathers, and his testimonies which he testified against them; and they followed vanity, and became vain, and went after the heathen that were round about them, concerning whom the Lord had charged them, that they should not do like them. And they left all the commandments of the Lord their God, and made them molten images, even two calves, and made a grove, and worshipped all the host of heaven, and served Baal. And they caused their sons and their daughters to pass through the fire, and used divination and enchantments, and sold themselves to do evil in the sight of the Lord, to provoke him to anger. Therefore the Lord was very angry with Israel, and removed them out of his sight: there was none left but the tribe of Judah only." (II Kings 17: 7-18.)

In this statement by the writer of the records of the kings of Israel we have irrefutable evidence substantiating the distinction made in the Bible between the House of Israel and the House of Judah. Israel was carried away into Assyrian captivity, as Hosea had warned, because of their failure to heed and obey the commandments, stat-

utes and judgments of the Lord. But this is not the end of
the story the Bible tells about the House of Israel. Although they vanished from sight in the records of Biblical
history, they appear again later in secular history, fulfilling all that the prophets predicted concerning their ultimate restoration to God's favor when they shall again live
in His sight.

CHAPTER III

The Acceptable Time

ECAUSE ISRAEL had forgotten God and had gone after her "lovers," the people were carried away into Assyrian captivity, for God had given them a bill of divorcement and sent them away. Yet, although the Lord was very angry with His people and had driven them from their land, through Moses He had previously declared:

> "And yet for all that, when they be in the land of their enemies, I will not cast them away, neither will I abhor them, to destroy them utterly, and to break my covenant with them: for I am the Lord their God. But I will for their sakes remember the covenant of their ancestors, whom I brought forth out of the land of Egypt in the sight of the heathen, that I might be their God: I am the Lord." (Lev. 26: 44-45.)

A NEW GENERATION

The statement, "remember the covenant of their ancestors," is a clear indication that this message was addressed to a generation far removed from the generation that Moses led out of the land of Egypt. Through Isaiah the Lord declares He will have mercy upon His people:

> "For a small moment have I forsaken thee; but with great mercies will I gather thee. In a little wrath I hid my

face from thee for a moment; but with everlasting kindness will I have mercy on thee, saith the Lord thy Redeemer." (Isa. 54: 7-8.)

That it is the House of Israel divorced, the woman forsaken and sent away, of whom the Lord is here speaking is made clear in the following two verses:

"For thy Maker is thine husband; the Lord of hosts is his name; and thy Redeemer the Holy One of Israel; the God of the whole earth shall he be called. For the Lord hath called thee as a woman forsaken and grieved in spirit, and a wife of youth, when thou wast refused, saith thy God." (Isa. 54: 5-6.)

Hosea depicts the moves God is to make to restore Israel to His favor again. Through this prophet the Lord declares:

"Therefore, behold, I will allure her, and bring her into the wilderness, and speak comfortably unto her." (Hosea 2: 14.)

It is this same wilderness to which reference is made by Ezekiel, where God declared He would plead with His people following the period when His fury would be poured out upon them for their sins:

"And I will bring you into the wilderness of the people, and there will I plead with you face to face. Like as I pleaded with your fathers in the wilderness of the land of Egypt, so will I plead with you, saith the Lord God." (Ez. 20: 35-36.)

In a footnote in *The Companion Bible,* the following statement is made about this wilderness:

"The wilderness of the people! Probably another country which would be to them another wilderness in which they were tested as to whether they would hear."

Does history record that the House of Israel moved out of Assyrian captivity into a wilderness? Esdras gives a most interesting account of just such a move on the part of Israel, whom he identifies as fulfilling their part in prophecy at a later date:

"Those are the ten tribes, which were carried away prisoners out of their own land in the time of Osea the king, whom Salmanasar the king of Assyria led away captive, and he carried them over the waters, and so came they into another land. But they took this counsel among themselves, that they would leave the multitude of the heathen, and go forth into a further country, where never mankind dwelt. That they might there keep their statutes, which they never kept in their own land. And they entered into Euphrates by the narrow passages of the river. For the most High then shewed signs for them, and held still the flood, till they were passed over. For through that country there was a great way to go, namely, of a year and a half: and the same region is called Arsareth." (II Esdras 13: 40-45.)

VALLEY OF ACHOR

When the House of Israel moved out of the land of Assyria and began their great westward trek, Hosea declares Israel was being "allured" into the wilderness. There God was to speak comfortably to her and provide for her needs. There also the "Valley of Achor" was to become a door of hope. Hosea tells of the beginning of the Divine pressure the purpose of which would be to compel Israel to move westward, bringing to pass the fulfillment of His word and the awakening of His people to acknowledge their identity and responsibility as His Kingdom people so that they might keep the terms of His covenant.

The reference to the Valley of Achor is significant, for it was in this valley that Achan, and all his family, were stoned to death because Achan had coveted wealth and had stolen gold and silver from Jericho, in defiance of the command of God, after Israel had taken that city (Joshua 7: 20-26). This act of covetousness on the part of Achan had caused the defeat of Israel before the city of Ai. The meaning of Achor is *trouble*. By referring to this valley, Hosea was alluding to the fact that the very trouble that had come upon Israel, bringing about their captivity, to be followed by their move into the wilderness, would ultimately be turned into a door of hope, for there the people were to be restored to happiness again:

"And she shall sing there, as in the days of her youth, and as in the day when she came up out of the land of Egypt." (Hosea 2: 15.)

THE WILDERNESS

It must not be overlooked that the territory designated as the wilderness into which God declared Israel was to be allured was not confined to the then uninhabited parts of southern and central Europe. That wilderness, which did include this unpopulated part of Europe, was, nevertheless, far more extensive and stretched westward to include the North American Continent. In the article, "North and West," DESTINY for November 1947 (pp. 363 & 369-371), Mr. Robert Swanton clearly demonstrated, by the projection of the north and west directional lines of Isaiah 49: 12, that Israel's wanderings, as they trekked westward to the "appointed place," not only embraced parts of Europe and the isles of the sea, but within those boundaries lies the North American Continent as well. Thus they include the United States of America and Canada. The bounds of that territory were actually set in ancient times according to Moses (Deut. 32: 8):

34

"A study of the accompanying maps [published with the above-mentioned article] . . . with the explanation given in Mr. Swanton's letter, demonstrates the accuracy of Isaiah's prophecy, as well as the significance of the statement made by Moses. Furthermore, this is the answer to the critics who object to the use of the reference to the north and west made by Isaiah to locate the appointed place— the territory in which Israel was to expand in fulfillment of prophecy. Taken literally, Isaiah has defined a large section of the globe beginning at a point in or near Palestine, bounded on one side by a line running north and on the other by a line running at right angles to this north directional line but going west until both lines meet at a given point in the Pacific Ocean, a point about half way between the west coast of the United States and the Hawaiian Islands."

BEGINNING OF ACCEPTABLE TIME

This is the wilderness into which God enticed His people and centuries have been consumed in that process. The valuable record in the thirteenth chapter of II Esdras describes only the beginning of the westward trek of the ten tribes. After residing for a time in Arsareth, they moved through southern and central Europe at different times and under different names throughout the centuries that followed. Ultimately they reached the isles north and west of Palestine, but the westward trek did not stop even there. From those isles as a gathering place, they again turned toward the west, taking possession of the desolate heritages of the North American Continent in fulfillment of Isaiah's prophecy:

"Thus saith the Lord, In an acceptable time have I heard thee, and in a day of salvation have I helped thee: and I will preserve thee, and give thee for a covenant of the people, to establish the earth, to cause to inherit the desolate heritages." (Isa. 49: 8.)

It is highly significant that the Lord specifies that this will take place "in an acceptable time," a period defined also as "a day of salvation." This indicates that there would be a set time when the Lord would begin to recognize His people. The statement is most striking in the light of the fact that it designates that *not until the Acceptable Year of the Lord had come could the acceptable time begin for the House of Israel.*

Thus, *the acceptable time* for the House of Israel, mentioned in Isaiah 49: 8, is definitely associated with *the Acceptable Year,* mentioned in Isaiah 61: 2, when the Redeemer of Israel was to begin His ministry, leading to the making of the required sacrifice that would redeem His people from the curse of the law of divorcement that separated them from their God. This is made clear by the statement that "the acceptable time" is inseparably linked with "the day of salvation," for it was only by the coming of the Saviour that their redemption and salvation were made certain.

When Jesus was in the synagogue on the Sabbath Day, there was delivered to Him the scroll of the Prophet Isaiah and He read:

"The Spirit of the Lord is upon me, because he hath anointed me to preach the gospel to the poor; he hath sent me to heal the brokenhearted, to preach deliverance to the captives, and recovering of sight to the blind, to set at liberty them that are bruised, to preach the acceptable year of the Lord." (Luke 4: 18-19.)

When this work was finished and He had died upon the cross and had risen from the grave, "the acceptable time" could begin for the House of Israel. The day of salvation had come. The captives whom He was to deliver as the Redeemer of Israel could now be set free. Knowing all this, and anticipating the coming day when, as the result of the finished work of redemption, the House of Israel must be told that they had been set free from the curse of the law, Jesus commissioned His disciples to go to them when He said:

> "Go not into the way of the Gentiles, and into any city of the Samaritans enter ye not: But go rather to the lost sheep of the house of Israel. And as ye go, preach, saying, The kingdom of heaven is at hand." (Matt. 10: 5-7.)

Why did Jesus especially direct His disciples to go to the House of Israel with the message of the Gospel of the Kingdom? It was because the Jews were to reject Him and the Kingdom was to be taken from them and given to a nation that would bring forth the fruits of the Kingdom. That nation was the House of Israel. The Jews were warned of this coming transfer:

> "Therefore say I unto you, The kingdom of God shall be taken from you, and given to a nation bringing forth the fruits thereof." (Matt. 21: 43.)

The New Covenant

The redemptive work of our Lord made it possible for the House of Israel to be the recipients of the Kingdom, for, as their Redeemer, Jesus Christ nullified the bill of divorcement by His own death. By this act He sealed the terms of the New Covenant with His blood, making it possible for His people to be reconciled to God through Him. Jeremiah stated the terms of the New Covenant, and they are also restated in Hebrews 8: 8-12:

> "Behold, the days come, saith the Lord, that I will make a new covenant with the house of Israel, and with the house of Judah: not according to the covenant that I made with their fathers in the day that I took them by the hand to

bring them out of the land of Egypt; which my covenant they brake, although I was an husband unto them, saith the Lord: But this shall be the covenant that I will make with the house of Israel; After those days, saith the Lord, I will put my law in their inward parts, and write it in their hearts; and will be their God, and they shall be my people." (Jer. 31: 31-33.)

Thus, "the Acceptable Year" inaugurated "the acceptable time" and Paul makes a specific announcement of the arrival of the latter:

"For he saith, I have heard thee in a time accepted, and in the day of salvation have I succoured thee: behold, now is the accepted [acceptable] time; behold, now is the day of salvation." (II Cor. 6: 2.)

CHILDREN OF THE MOTHER

In anticipation of the day when the House of Israel would be free from the curse of this law, the Lord, through Isaiah the Prophet, speaks to the children of the mother to whom the bill of divorcement had been given. Because this message is directed to the children of the divorced wife, and Israel, not Judah, was divorced, then it is to the descendants of Israel, not Judah, to whom the Lord is speaking through the Prophet Isaiah:

"Thus saith the Lord, Where is the bill of your mother's divorcement, whom I have put away? Or which of my creditors is it to whom I have sold you?" (Isa. 50: 1.)

After asking these challenging questions, the Lord declares:

"Behold, for your iniquities have ye sold yourselves, and for your transgressions is your mother put away." (Isa. 50: 1.)

The burden of Hosea's messages directed to the northern ten-tribed Kingdom of the House of Israel was their iniquities, which would inevitably eventuate in their divorcement from God who was sending them away for their sins. In their divorced state the situation seemed to be utterly hopeless and, recognizing the inability of Israel to extricate herself from her predicament, the Lord asks:

"Wherefore, when I came, was there no man? When I called, was there none to answer?" (Isa. 50: 2.)

It is the Lord as the Messiah and Redeemer who is speaking here and in the expression, "When I came," we have a reference to His first advent. John points to the fulfillment of this promised coming when he records:

"He came unto his own, and his own received him not." (John 1: 11.)

Thus "He came" as predicted and, by the lack of response on the part of the Nation of the Jews to that coming, no one answered. However, the very fact of their refusal to answer by accepting Him as their Messiah, which brought about His rejection, answered the next question:

"Is my hand shortened at all, that it cannot redeem? Or have I no power to deliver?" (Isa. 50: 2.)

This is followed by a recitation of the mighty works of the Lord which demonstrate His power. Reference is made to the drying up of the sea and the turning of rivers into a desert. He speaks also of turning the heavens into blackness as the storms rage. As the Messiah, the servant of the Lord, who is able to deliver, He sets forth His qualifications:

"The Lord God hath given me the tongue of the learned, that I should know how to speak a word in season to him that is weary." (Isa. 50: 4.)

Smith and Goodspeed translate this:

"The Lord God has given me a tongue for teaching that I may know how to succor the weary with a word."

Referring to His willingness to obey and fulfill the assigned task, He declares:

"The Lord God has opened my ear, and I have not been rebellious, I have not turned backward." (Isa. 50: 5, *Smith & Goodspeed Trans.*)

Having set forth His qualifications to teach and His acceptance of the assigned task, the Messiah now shows the type of reception He will receive when He begins the work of redeeming His people:

"I gave my back to the smiters, and my cheeks to the pluckers of hair; my face I hid not from shame and spitting." (Isa. 50: 6, *Smith & Goodspeed Trans.*)

As the Messiah He now states the source of His help and strength:

"But the Lord God helps me, therefore I have not been confounded; I have set my face like a flint, and I know that I shall not be ashamed." (Isa. 50: 7, *Smith & Goodspeed Trans.*)

His death was a prearranged event and He accomplished it Himself. This was made clear when, on the Mount of Transfiguration, Jesus Christ talked with Moses and Elijah:

"And, behold, there talked with him two men, which were Moses and Elias [Elijah]: who appeared in glory, and spake of his decease which he should accomplish at Jerusalem." (Luke 9: 30-31.)

Jesus Himself declared:

"I lay down my life, that I might take it again. No man taketh it from me, but I lay it down of myself. I have power to lay it down, and I have power to take it again. This commandment have I received of my Father." (John 10: 17-18.)

The reference to setting His face like a flint was fulfilled when the hour had come:

"And it came to pass, when the time was come that he should be received up, he stedfastly set his face to go to Jerusalem." (Luke 9: 51.)

Through Isaiah the Messiah declares God will vindicate Him and He asks who will contend with Him, calling upon him to stand up and show himself. Who is the adversary, He inquires, who can convict Him of lawlessness? Let him come near.

Isaiah then admonishes those who fear the Lord to obey the voice of His Servant. Even though they walk in darkness and have no light, they may trust in Him and rely upon their God. Those who are evil and treacherous, so the prophet declares, will have sorrow and torment.

In the light of Hosea's statement that God would speak words of comfort to Israel in the wilderness; that is, He will speak to her heart, a call for Israel to hearken is given through Isaiah following the announcement of the Messiah's determination to redeem His people:

"Hearken to me, ye that follow after righteousness, ye that seek the Lord." (Isa. 51: 1.)

Smith and Goodspeed render this:

"Listen to me, you who press after deliverance, you who seek the Lord!"

That this message is addressed to the House of Israel, not Judah, is made clear by the context, for the call is to a people who have completely forgotten that they are the descendants of Abraham and that Sarah was their mother. The 51st and 52nd chapters of Isaiah contain words of comfort addressed to the divorced wife, calling upon her to listen, to awaken and to return, for the days of her troubles were coming to an end:

"Thus saith thy Lord the LORD, and thy God that pleadeth the cause of his people, Behold, I have taken out of thine hand the cup of trembling, even the dregs of the cup of my fury; thou shalt no more drink it again: But I will put it into the hand of them that afflict thee." (Isa. 51: 22-23.)

The certainty of their redemption is set forth in the following statement:

"For thus saith the Lord, Ye have sold yourselves for nought; and ye shall be redeemed without money." (Isa. 52: 3.)

Referring to the ultimate accomplishments by the Messiah, their Redeemer, the Lord declares:

"Lo! my servant shall prosper, He shall be exalted, and lifted up, and shall be very high. As many were amazed at him—so marred was his appearance beyond that of a man, and his form beyond that of the sons of men—so shall he startle many nations, on account of him kings shall shut their mouths; for what has not been told them shall they see, and what they have not heard shall they contemplate." (Isa. 52: 13-15, *Smith & Goodspeed Trans.*)

Following this glorious prediction of the greatness of the Messiah and His Kingdom, when the kings of the earth will pay homage to Him, Isaiah vividly describes His coming passion, which was fulfilled in the suffering and death of Jesus Christ, by which means He redeemed His people and brought salvation to all who will accept Him as Saviour. The Lord had previously challenged His people to say whether His hand was shortened so that it could not redeem. Now the questions are asked:

"Who hath believed our report? And to whom is the arm of the Lord revealed?" (Isa. 53: 1.)

Then he declares:

"He was wounded for our transgressions, he was bruised for our iniquities: the chastisement of our peace was upon him; and with his stripes we are healed. . . . The Lord hath laid on him the iniquity of us all." (Isa. 53: 5-6.)

THE EXPANSION OF ISRAEL

It has already been pointed out that a woman was bound under the marriage law so long as her husband lived. God had entered into a symbolic relationship of marriage with His people, so the only way the House of Israel could escape the penalty of the law under which she had been divorced from God was to have the bill of divorcement blotted out by the death of Him who had written it. The 53rd chapter of Isaiah foretells the accomplishment of this redemption, after which the prophet records the effect all this will have upon the House of Israel:

"Sing, O barren, thou that didst not bear; break forth into singing, and cry aloud, thou that didst not travail with child: for more are the children of the desolate than the children of the married wife, saith the Lord." (Isa. 54: 1.)

Hosea declared that in the wilderness Israel would sing again as in the days of her youth and Isaiah here confirms this fact as a result of their redemption. After their deliverance from the curse of the law, they were now to expand and grow in numbers far more so than Judah, the "married wife":

> "Enlarge the site of your tent, and stretch without limit the curtains of your home; Lengthen your cords, and make fast your pegs! For to right and to left shall you spread abroad, and your descendants shall take over the heritage of the nations, And shall people the desolate cities. Fear not! For you shall not be put to shame; And be not confounded! For you shall not be put to shame. The shame of your youth shall you forget, and the reproach of your widowhood shall you remember no more." (Isa. 54: 2-4, *Smith & Goodspeed Trans.*)

The troubles which had caused the House of Israel to be sent into captivity, and then forced them to move westward from the land of their captors, brought them into a place where ultimate blessing awaited them. The Prophet Jeremiah had foretold this development:

> "Thus saith the Lord, The people which were left of the sword found grace in the wilderness; even Israel, when I went to cause him to rest." (Jer. 31: 2.)

Eventually they were to experience release from the restraints which had retarded their free movement and they were to engage in colonial expansion on a scale never before known. However, this was not until the Bible had become an Open Book among them, when, as the result of the invention of the printing press, the real work of colonization commenced. It was during the Protestant Reformation, through the publication and distribution of the Bible in the language of the people, that the building of a new civilization began, based upon the equity and righteousness of the Divine law (See *Study in Revelation*, pp. 100-117*).

Society in the sixteenth and seventeenth centuries, particularly during the Elizabethan Period, was agitated to its profoundest depths by the great religious insurrection within Anglo-Saxondom. The House of Israel was thus being spiritually prepared to go out and take possession of their larger inheritance, carrying with them the Book that would give guidance and direction in their undertakings. This in itself is a most remarkable identification mark of the origin and destiny of the people of the House of Israel, whom the Lord heard "in the acceptable time."

The colonization of America followed as a result of the religious convulsions stemming from the Reformation. But the enemies of His Kingdom could not resist making a supreme attempt at this time to interfere with their mission and, if possible, destroy the Open Book. The Spanish Armada was equipped and launched with this objective in mind, but by the utter destruction of this great Armada during the reign of Queen Elizabeth I, the enemy was blocked from interfering further with the onward march of the Kingdom people.

FREED FROM IDOLATRY

No longer harassed by the enemies who had formerly beset them, and entirely free from contact with the Baal worshippers of former days who had been their neighbors in Palestine, modern Israel, the Anglo-Saxon-Celtic peoples, took possession of the appointed place of their inheritance north and west of Palestine. Foreseeing all this, Hosea exclaimed:

* $3.50 postpaid. Destiny Publishers, Haverhill, Mass.

"And it shall be at that day, saith the Lord, that thou shalt call me Ishi; and shall call me no more Baali." (Hosea 2: 16.)

Isaiah declares of Israel, "Thy Maker is thine husband." For Israel to call the Lord "Ishi" is for them to recognize the close relationship existing between them and their God. One interesting interpretation of the word "Ishi" is *My man husband* which, in the light of the statement by Isaiah, could very readily refer to Him who was to be born of a virgin and called Immanuel; that is, *God (is) with us.* The people of Israel, living in the appointed place, acknowledge this to be a reality in their services of worship and praise:

"For unto us a child is born, unto us a son is given: and the government shall be upon his shoulder: and his name shall be called Wonderful, Counsellor, The mighty God, The everlasting Father, The Prince of Peace. Of the increase of his government and peace there shall be no end, upon the throne of David, and upon his kingdom, to order it, and to establish it with judgment and with justice from henceforth even for ever. The zeal of the Lord of hosts will perform this." (Isa. 9: 6-7.)

The Lord sent a Word into Jacob, but it failed to remain there (Isa. 9: 8), for Jesus Christ, the Word made flesh (John 1: 14), came to Judea and was rejected by the Jews. However, the Word did alight upon Israel, for the Gospel was carried to the isles of the sea where Christianity took root and, as a result, the Anglo-Saxon-Celtic peoples were Christianized and have been moving on toward the goal set for His Israel peoples in these last days. The ultimate result will be that they will awaken to the realization that their Maker is their Husband, Lord, Redeemer and King, for they no longer refer to Baal as their master or lord. This is the complete fulfillment of Hosea's statement:

> "For I will take away the names of Baalim out of her mouth, and they shall no more be remembered by their name." (Hosea 2: 17.)

Ferrar Fenton translates this:

> "And I will take the names of her 'Masters,' from her mouth and she will no longer remember their names."

Even the names by which the gods of the land were served in ancient times are no longer remembered in modern Israel. But this is only the beginning of the work that will be accomplished as God moves to compel His people to acknowledge that they are the people of His Kingdom and brings them into wholehearted accord with the requirements of His laws. The ultimate end will be the full restoration spoken of by all the prophets, when peace will be established throughout the earth. Israel shall then be rebetrothed to God in righteousness, in faithfulness and in loving-kindness forever.

CHAPTER IV

A Promised Deliverance

IN THE preceding chapter it was pointed out that modern Israel no longer remembers the names of the gods their ancestors worshipped. Through Hosea the Prophet the Lord declared that in the day this became true He would make a covenant in behalf of His people with the beasts of the field, with the fowls of the air and with the creeping things of the ground. This allusion to such a covenant is a reference to the time when the full restoration of His people to their preordained status in His plan will become a reality. Isaiah also referred to this same covenant:

"The wolf also shall dwell with the lamb, and the leopard shall lie down with the kid; and the calf and the young lion and the fatling together; and a little child shall lead them. And the cow and the bear shall feed; their young ones shall lie down together: and the lion shall eat straw like the ox. And the sucking child shall play on the hole of the asp, and the weaned child shall put his hand on the cockatrice' [adder's] den. They shall not hurt nor destroy in all my holy mountain: for the earth shall be full of the knowledge of the Lord, as the waters cover the sea." (Isa. 11: 6-9.)

48

COVENANT OF PEACE

All this will come to pass following the restoration when, as stated by the Lord through Ezekiel:

> "I will set up one shepherd over them, and he shall feed them, even my servant David; he shall feed them, and he shall be their shepherd. And I the Lord will be their God, and my servant David a prince among them; I the Lord have spoken it. And I will make with them a covenant of peace, and will cause the evil beasts to cease out of the land: and they shall dwell safely in the wilderness, and sleep in the woods." (Ez. 34: 23-25.)

Hosea's next prediction establishes a definite time when this is to be accomplished, for it is only as a consequence of the restoration that the prophecy will be fulfilled:

> "And I will break the bow and the sword and the battle out of the earth, and will make them to lie down safely." (Hosea 2: 18.)

Both Isaiah and Micah confirm this, for these prophets predict that conflicts and wars will cease only after the Kingdom has been exalted. The statement is:

> "The mountain of the house of the Lord shall be established in the top of the mountains, and it shall be exalted above the hills; and people shall flow unto it." (Micah 4: 1; see also Isa. 2: 2.)

When the Kingdom of God is fully established in a place of eminence over all kingdoms, and exalted above all governments, there will be an irresistible desire on the part of peoples to partake of the prosperity of its administration. The nations will say:

> "Come, and let us go up to the mountain of the Lord, and to the house of the God of Jacob; and he will teach us of his ways, and we will walk in his paths." (Micah 4: 2.)

Having learned about the benefits of a righteous administration as a result of coming to the Kingdom—an entirely voluntary move on the part of the surrounding nations—the fulfillment of Micah's prediction will be the result:

"The law shall go forth of Zion, and the word of the Lord from Jerusalem." (Micah 4: 2.)

The final outcome will confirm the Covenant of Peace:

"He shall judge among many people, and rebuke strong nations afar off; and they shall beat their swords into plowshares, and their spears into pruninghooks: nation shall not lift up a sword against nation, neither shall they learn war any more." (Micah 4: 3.)

PROCESS OF TIME

The process of time involved to bring about the fulfillment of all of these prophecies was to commence after God's people had forgotten the names of the gods their forefathers worshipped. Then God would begin the work of restoration. This would follow the completion of the "days of Baalim," as pointed out in Chapter II. Israel had served Baal for 360 years and, according to the judgment pronounced upon them, they must come under chastisement for "seven times" the number of years they had worshipped Baal before they would again be eligible to function as God's Kingdom under the terms of the "If" clauses of the National Covenant God made with them at Mt. Sinai.

The years of the chastisement of the House of Israel did not begin to expire until 1551-1552 A.D. They were then living under another name in the Isles of the Sea, i.e., the British Isles. A movement toward a return to a pure form of worship began among them; images were removed from the churches and the doctrine of transubstantiation was rejected. By 1601-1668 A.D., the Puritan Movement had developed and responsible government was established. It was the time of the beginning of the increase in England's power, her colonial expansion and the colonization of America. The people of God began to spread abroad over the face of the earth, inheriting the desolate heritages and occupying waste places.

During those years a genuine revival in spiritual religion was coincident with great advancements in industry and commerce. By 1800-1802 A.D., Napoleon was defeated in Egypt, blocking his plans and opening the way for an era of remarkable expansion for both England and the United States. The days of Baalim were fulfilled and the work of restoration was under way.* In Hosea's book this is all expressed in terms of the rebetrothal of His people to the Lord:

"And I will betroth thee unto me for ever; yea, I will betroth thee unto me in righteousness, and in judgment, and in lovingkindness, and in mercies. I will even betroth thee unto me in faithfulness: and thou shalt know the Lord." (Hosea 2: 19-20.)

STEPS IN REBETROTHAL

Immediately following the ending of the first stage in the Seven Times of punishment, the Lord began to rebetroth His people to Himself, first in faithfulness, reversing the order of the steps in the rebetrothal as they are given in Hosea 2: 19-20. This was evidenced in the renewal of spiritual religion, leading to the fulfillment of Hosea's declaration, "and thou shalt know the Lord." It

* See Plate 16 in *Primogenesis* by Howard B. Rand. $5.00 postpaid, Destiny Publishers, Haverhill, Mass.

was the result of the spiritual awakening that swept over Anglo-Saxondom, leading to the great missionary movements of the early nineteenth century. Throughout that same century the Church manifested the spirit of the Church of Philadelphia, one of the seven Church Periods of the Book of Revelation, before whom an open door had been set, for they kept His word and did not deny His name (Rev. 3: 7-8).

But Hosea declared that God would betroth Israel to Him forever, which of necessity presupposes the fact that His people, who had lost all knowledge of their identity, will awaken to the realization of who they are. What do we find to be true? During the same time that the House of Israel, the Anglo-Saxon-Celtic peoples, were being aroused to spiritual requirements, the call was also going out to them to acknowledge their origin in fulfillment of Isaiah's message:

"Hearken to me, ye that follow after righteousness, ye that seek the Lord: look unto the rock whence ye are hewn, and to the hole of the pit whence ye are digged. Look unto Abraham your father, and unto Sarah that bare you." (Isa. 51: 1-2.)

This message is addressed to a people who, although they are seeking the Lord, do not know they are Israel or that Abraham was their father and Sarah their mother. The call is to urge them to look to their origin and identify themselves with their ancestors. They must come to realize that they are the descendants of Abraham and, therefore, they are the House of Israel in the world today. The identity proclamation has been going out in ever-increasing volume throughout the Anglo-Saxon-Celtic world during the last century until today millions are aware of their origin and identity.

BETROTHED IN RIGHTEOUSNESS

Few, however, have become cognizant as yet of the responsibilities assigned to the House of Israel. Nevertheless, their awakening to what is required of them as God's people is next on the agenda. It is in this connection that Hosea declares that, in the process of restoring Israel to God's favor again, He will betroth them unto Himself in righteousness. Once their origin has been acknowledged and their identity established, the next step is to proclaim their responsibility to God under the terms of the covenant He made with them at Mount Sinai.

It was there that their forefathers said, "All that the Lord hath spoken we will do" (Ex. 19: 8). At that time the people affirmed their intention to be obedient and observe the requirements of the Law of the Lord. It is these laws modern Israel must restore and obey in fulfillment of the oath taken by their forefathers. When this finally becomes a reality, the betrothal in righteousness will become a fact and Ezekiel's prediction will come to pass:

"And I will put my spirit within you, and cause you to walk in my statutes, and ye shall keep my judgments, and do them." (Ez. 36: 27.)

Then judgment, loving-kindness and mercies will be major attributes of a righteous people. Through Isaiah the Prophet a call is issued, exhorting God's people to submit themselves to God and to this sanctification as a nation:

"Thus saith the Lord, Keep ye judgment, and do justice: for my salvation is near to come, and my righteousness to be revealed." (Isa. 56: 1.)

53

NATURE IN HARMONY

When God's people have become "all righteous," as Isaiah puts it (Isa. 60: 21), God will move in a marvelous manner to restore harmony in nature for their sake:

> "It shall come to pass in that day, I will hear, saith the Lord, I will hear the heavens, and they shall hear the earth; and the earth shall hear the corn, and the wine, and the oil; and they shall hear Jezreel." (Hosea 2: 21-22.)

This denotes that there will be a perfect synchronization in nature, for the willing compliance with the Divine will will set those laws in motion that will bring the earth in tune with the infinite purpose. The harmony in "hearing" denotes that there will be no discord throughout all of God's creation, for His will shall be done on earth as it is done in heaven. The result will be that the earth will yield her increase, fulfilling the law:

> "I will give you rain in due season, and the land shall yield her increase, and the trees of the field shall yield their fruit. And your threshing shall reach unto the vintage, and the vintage shall reach unto the sowing time: and ye shall eat your bread to the full, and dwell in your land safely." (Lev. 26: 4-5.)

This promise is predicated upon the assumption that His people will walk according to His precepts and obey all of His commandments. Joel refers to such a day coming when the blessings of abundance will be poured out upon His people. It will be at a time when, because of their distress, the people will turn to their Lord and ask for His help. Then Joel declares:

> "Yea, the Lord will answer and say unto his people, Behold, I will send you corn, and wine, and oil, and ye shall

be satisfied therewith: and I will no more make you a reproach among the heathen." (Joel 2: 19.)

JEZREEL

The Lord's words through the prophet (Hos. 2: 21-22), therefore, show this aspect of the restoration to be characterized by the rhythm of renewal, like a thrilling cadence rising to a resounding climax: *"And they shall hear Jezreel!"* The significant import of the word "Jezreel" was pointed out in Chapter I, in which it was shown that the Great Day of Jezreel will be the Great Day of God's Harvest, *i.e.,* God's harvest time when those who sleep in the dust of the earth shall awaken in fulfillment of Isaiah's prophecy:

> "Awake and sing, ye that dwell in dust: for thy dew is as the dew of herbs." (Isa. 26: 19.)

It must not be overlooked that from the dust of the earth there will come an awakening of the dead who are to arise in triumphant resurrection and furnish leadership in the restored Kingdom.* This is made clear from the exclamation following the statement in Revelation that the resurrected ones are to occupy thrones in His Kingdom:

> "Blessed and holy is he that hath part in the first resurrection: on such the second death hath no power, but they shall be priests [administrators] of God and of Christ, and shall reign with him a thousand years." (Rev. 20: 6.)

A SYMBOLIC TERM

The concluding verse of the second chapter of Hosea is

---

* See "The Summons to the Rulers," *Documentary Studies,* Vol. III, pp. 408-412. $5.00 postpaid (Vols. I, II & III available; any two, $9.50; all three, $13.95), Destiny Publishers, Haverhill, Mass.

an assertion by the Lord that His endeavors to win His people back to Himself will be successful:

> "And I will sow her unto me in the earth; and I will have mercy upon her that had not obtained mercy; and I will say to them which were not my people, Thou art my people; and they shall say, Thou art my God." (Hosea 2: 23.)

It is important to note that the statement, "And I will sow her unto me in the earth," immediately follows the declaration, "And they shall hear Jezreel. Moffatt translates the opening statement of the 23rd verse, "I will re-people Jezreel in the land." Thus, *Jezreel*, which means "God sows," becomes a symbolic term, referring to the seed which God has sown in the earth, *i.e.*, those who are destined to come forth from their graves in the day of resurrection. That these dead were sown in the earth is so stated by Paul, who said:

> "There is one glory of the sun, and another glory of the moon, and another glory of the stars: for one star differeth from another star in glory. So also is the resurrection of the dead. It is sown in corruption: it is raised in incorruption: It is sown in dishonour; it is raised in glory: it is sown in weakness; it is raised in power: It is sown a natural body; it is raised a spiritual body. . . . In a moment, in the twinkling of an eye, at the last trump: for the trumpet shall sound, and the dead shall be raised incorruptible." (I Cor. 15: 41-44 and 52.)

These resurrected ones are those specifically referred to when the Lord states, "I will sow her *unto me* in the earth." This is the new Israel of God, a select planting that will insure a harvest of righteousness in the new age. Using other terms, the same thought is expressed through Malachi:

"And they shall be mine, saith the Lord of hosts, in that day when I make up my jewels; and I will spare them, as a man spareth his own son that serveth him. Then shall ye return, and discern between the righteous and the wicked, between him that serveth God and him that serveth him not." (Mal. 3: 17-18.)

It will be impossible for the restoration of the administration of the perfect Law of the Lord to be complete until those who are to rule in the restored Kingdom have been summoned and have arisen from their graves to take their assigned places. The assumption of office of these rulers will bring into complete harmony the administration of the affairs of the Kingdom of God on earth with that of heaven. Thus will Isaiah's prediction be fulfilled:

"I will also make thy officers peace, and thine exactors righteousness. Violence shall no more be heard in thy land, wasting nor destruction within thy borders; but thou shalt call thy walls Salvation, and thy gates Praise . . . the Lord shall be thine everlasting light, and the days of thy mourning shall be ended." (Isa. 60: 17-18 and 20.)

Hosea began his message with the pronouncement of no mercy upon the House of Israel, who were to become *Lo-Ammi*, "not My people," as a result of their turning away from God to serve Baal. Now he declares that when God has accomplished the completion of the rebetrothal to Himself of His people, named *Lo-Ruhamah*, who had previously not obtained mercy, they will become *Ammi*, "Thou art my people." In that day Hosea depicts the whole nation with one voice as saying to the Lord, "Thou art my God." Zechariah's prophecy provides additional confirmation of this:

"And they shall be my people, and I will be their God, in truth and in righteousness. . . . They shall call on my name, and I will hear them: I will say, It is my people: and they shall say, The Lord is my God." (Zech. 8: 8; 13: 9.)

This glorious reunion and restatement of vows will be followed by the promised prosperity:

"For the seed shall be prosperous; the vine shall give her fruit, and the ground shall give her increase, and the heavens shall give their dew; and I will cause the remnant of this people to possess all these things." (Zech. 8: 12.)

THE PROPHET'S PREVIEW

In the first two chapters of his book, Hosea tells the story of the rejection, the punishment, the regathering and the ultimate restoration of the House of Israel. In one bold sweep across the centuries of time, beginning with the dispersion of the House of Israel and climaxing in their redemption, the resurrection of their rulers and the restoration of the Kingdom, followed by universal peace and prosperity, the prophet provides a telescopic preview of the march of the House of Israel through the pages of history. Having presented the over-all blueprint of Israel's future, the prophet then proceeds to give in more detail the conditions which made the great captivity inevitable.

CHAPTER V

Impending Judgment

HOSEA WAS next prepared, under further unusual personal circumstances, to pronounce God's judgment upon the House of Israel. This was to eventually culminate in a long period when they would be completely severed from all connection with their past, yet not forsaken by their God who still loved them. Hosea was told to again go and fall in love with a woman. This was not Gomer who had borne children to him as his wife and who apparently had died. It was to be a second marriage for Hosea and the prophet was to enter into this marriage in a way that would illustrate the relationship of God to His people during the long years of their chastisement because of their sins. The prophet was told:

> "Go, love a woman that is beloved of a paramour, and is an adulteress; even as the Lord loves the Israelites, though they turn to other gods and are lovers of raisincakes." (Hosea 3: 1, *Smith & Goodspeed Trans.*)

Moffatt translates this command:

> "Go again and love an adulterous woman, in love with a paramour."

The prophet was to select a woman from the northern tribes, for this is what is indicated by calling her an adulteress. The whole House of Israel was in love with their idolatrous practices, forsaking their God to worship the images of other gods. The "raisin-cakes" were a reference to offerings made to heathen gods and goddesses.

Following the instructions given him, Hosea purchased a woman for fifteen pieces of silver. This was the price paid for the redemption of a slave; therefore, an allusion to the enslaved condition of the House of Israel. Because God was soon to send Israel away, driving her into the wilderness where, under the circumstances imposed upon her, she would be completely separated from her "lovers," Hosea announced to the woman whom he had purchased:

"Many days you must dwell as mine; you must not play the harlot, nor have a husband; nor will I myself come near you." (Hosea 3: 3, *Smith & Goodspeed Trans.*)

Moffatt translates these orders:

"For many a day you must remain mine, you must not play the harlot, you must have nothing to do with a man— and I will have nothing to do with you."

Ferrar Fenton renders this:

"You shall stay long without me,—you shall not prostitute yourself, nor offer yourself to men,—and then I will be yours."

In this manner, in Hosea's own married life, he was to illustrate the many years of separation which were to occur between God and His people, during which period God declared He would not be a husband to Israel. However, it was made clear that, after the long period had passed, the relationship would change. Hosea told the woman that eventually his marriage to her would be consummated and this was an indication that eventually

Israel would be restored to their God. That this analogous meaning is intended is confirmed by Hosea's statement:

> "For the children of Israel shall abide many days without a king, and without a prince, and without a sacrifice, and without an image, and without an ephod, and without teraphim." (Hosea 3: 4.)

MANY DAYS

When the House of Israel was finally carried away into Assyrian captivity, they did not remain there permanently, for the breaking up of the Assyrian Empire gave them their opportunity to escape. From the land of their captors they moved north and west, thus beginning the "many days" during which they were to be without a king and without a prince. These were the years during which they wandered in the wilderness of central and southern Europe. Then, no doubt unknowingly impelled by their pre-ordained destiny, they took up their long trek westward as they journeyed toward the "appointed place" of which Nathan the Prophet had spoken when he communicated the words of the Lord to David:

> "Moreover I will appoint a place for my people Israel, and will plant them, that they may dwell in a place of their own, and move no more; neither shall the children of wickedness afflict them any more, as beforetime." (II Sam. 7: 10.)

In Chapters I to X of his book, *Chemivision,* Dr. William J. Hale traces the successive waves of this Israel trek westward toward the "appointed place" of which the British Isles were a part. The full extent of the territory thus assigned was not to be occupied until many generations later on since it included the North American Continent.

From the time that the House of Israel was taken captive into Assyria in 721 B.C., to their regathering in the Isles north and west of Palestine some centuries later, their entire mode of living completely changed. Former practices were abandoned, the sacrifices ceased and the priestly office became vacant. No idols of any kind were found among the wandering peoples and idolatry was no longer a characteristic of the House of Israel.

Hosea forecast the eventual outcome of all their wanderings after their arrival at their destination:

"Afterward shall the children of Israel return, and seek the Lord their God, and David their king; and shall fear the Lord and his goodness in the latter days." (Hosea 3: 5.)

Afterward

Afterward! Like the phrase, "many days," much is to be comprehended as taking place within the chronological bounds designated by the word "afterward." This period would bring about the fulfillment of the prediction of Hosea as set forth in his first chapter when the prophet declared:

"And it shall come to pass, that in the place where it was said unto them, Ye are not my people, there it shall be said unto them, Ye are the sons of the living God." (Hosea 1: 10.)

This statement was dealt with fully in Chapter I under the subtitle, *Sons of God,* showing that modern Israel would be known as a Christian people. That Christianity was taken directly to the people dwelling in the Isles is clear from a study of the historical evidence. Following the crucifixion and resurrection of Jesus Christ, the early apostles of the Church at Jerusalem carried the glad tidings of redemption to Israel in the Isles. A brief summary of the facts about this transfer of the Gospel from Palestine to the Isles north and west of that land was given in "Cradle of Christianity," DESTINY for April 1952, as follows:

"Christianity originated in Palestine and, when the center of activity moved from that land, it did not go to Rome but, hundreds of years before there was a Pope at Rome, it was transferred to the Isles of the North and West by Joseph of Arimathea and those who fled from Jerusalem and Palestine to escape persecution. They established the first church in the British Isles—only a few years after the crucifixion—at Glastonbury, England.

"Furthermore, we seriously question if the Apostle Peter ever visited Rome, for he was an apostle to Babylon (see I Peter 5: 13) where, in his time, many Jews were dwelling. There Peter no doubt suffered his martyrdom by being crucified. Paul went to Rome and there is abundant evidence that on one of his missionary journeys he also visited London where, from Ludgate Hill, he preached the Gospel. If Peter had been in Rome, Paul would certainly not have failed to include him in his greetings to the friends there. His very silence indicates that Peter was where he declares that he was in his Epistle: at Babylon. The claim of the sacred heritage of apostolic descent is hardly sustained in the lack of all evidence that Peter ever was at Rome.

"In spite of all this, and despite the fundamental fact that missionaries from Rome admittedly found a strong flourishing Christian Church in the British Isles, established centuries before their arrival, men continue to erroneously repeat the statement that Rome brought Christianity to the Isles. That city, once the center of the pagan Roman Empire, is now the center of the Papacy—a powerful politico-ecclesiastical organization—but never has it been the center of true Christianity from whence the House of Israel, the Anglo-Saxon-Celtic peoples, received the Gospel.

"When God called Israel to be His servant, He saw to it

63

that His Gospel, which Israel was to transmit, was taken directly to the Isles by the disciples of our Lord. His people Israel received their commission directly from Jerusalem, not by way of Rome, regardless of the claims of Rome and of those who accept those claims as true!

"Jesus commissioned His disciples to 'go unto the lost sheep of the House of Israel' and He constituted them the lightbearers of the Gospel to His people. When He said to the Jews, 'The kingdom of God shall be taken from you, and given to a nation bringing forth the fruits thereof,' it was to the House of Israel that the disciples carried the message and to Israel that the transfer of the Kingdom was made. The company of disciples and believers who, with Joseph of Arimathea, established the first Christian church in the Isles, were instruments in the hand of the Lord in accomplishing the transfer directly from Eastminster (Jerusalem) to Westminster in the Isles of the Sea north and west of Palestine.

"Our Lord did not wait hundreds of years, as taught by Rome, before giving Israel the glad tidings of their redemption, but sent the disciples directly to the Isles with the message of the Gospel. The conversion of England to Christianity is given in the *Encyclopaedia Britannica* as taking place between 597 and 686 A.D., but the following inscription in the Church of St. Peter-Upon-Cornhill, London, England is evidence that there was a flourishing Christian church in the Isles long before the Church of Rome was able to send emissaries to Britain—which it did not do until 597 A.D. when Pope Gregory the Great sent a mission to England headed by Augustine, who landed at Ebbsfleet in that year. Note this inscription carefully and mark the date:

" 'Bee it known to all men that in the year of Our Lord God 179 Lucives, the first Christian king of this Land, then called Britaine, founded ye first Church in London, that is to say, ye Church of St. Peter-Upon-Cornehill and hee founded there an Archbishop's See and made that Church ye Metropolitane and Chiefe Church of this kingdome and so it endured ye space of 400 years and more, unto the coming of St. Avstin the Apostle of England, the which was sent into this land by St. Gregorie, ye Doctor of ye Church, in the time of King Ethelbert and then was the Archbishop's See and Pall removed from ye said Church of St. Peter-Upon-Cornehill unto Dorobernia that now is called Canterburie and there it remaineth to this day and Millet, a monke which came into this land with St. Avstin, hee was made the first Bishop of London and his See was in Paul's Church and this Lucives king was the first founder of St. Peter's Church upon Cornehill and hee reigned king in this land after Brute 1245 yeares and in the yeares of our Lord God 124 Lucives was crowned king and hee was buried [After some Chronicles hee was buried at Gloucester in that place where ye order of St. Francis standeth now].'

"It is interesting to note the reference to Brute, or Brutus, who came to London after the destruction of Troy, for he was also of Israel stock.

"No nation or city outside of Israel's lands can rightly lay claim to being the true seat of Christianity. It is only logical to recognize that the origin of the Christian Church was in Palestine—where Jesus Christ lived and completed His work as the Redeemer of Israel and Saviour of the World. When the Gospel activities were transferred from that land, they went to another Israel land—to the Isles of the Sea. When the People of the Book recognize this, abundant light will be shed on their history and destiny."

Thus the seeds of the Gospel were planted among the Israel peoples and they took root in the Isles, with the result that the House of Israel ultimately returned to the Lord their God and sought His goodness. This very act fulfilled our Lord's words addressed to the Jews who rejected Him:

"The kingdom of God shall be taken from you, and given to a nation bringing forth the fruits thereof." (Matt. 21: 43.)

That nation was the House of Israel awaiting the reception of the glad tidings of redemption as they gathered together again in the appointed place. With the acceptance of Christianity came the fulfillment of Hosea's prediction that in the very place where they were considered to be "not God's people," they would be called "the sons of God" as the result of their acceptance of Jesus Christ as their Redeemer and Saviour.

PRECEDED BY THEIR KING

While the House of Israel was for many centuries without a king and without a prince, as foretold by Hosea, it was revealed through Micah the Prophet that their king would pass on before them. Careful research into the records of history proves this to be true and shows that their Davidic monarch was residing in the Isles of the Sea, awaiting their coming. It was also pointed out in Micah's remarkable prophecy that what remained of unity among them as the ten tribes of the House of Israel was broken up when they "passed through the gate," moving through the pass in the Caucasus Mountains that took them out of Asia and into Europe. Micah states:

> "The breaker is come up before them: they have broken up, and have passed through the gate, and are gone out by it: and their king shall pass before them, and the Lord on the head of them." (Micah 2: 13.)

Smith and Goodspeed render this passage:

> "And they shall go forth from Edom. The breaker shall go up before them; They shall break through the gate and go forth thereby; Their king shall pass on before them, With the Lord at their head."

Esdras confirms the fact that the House of Israel, *i.e.,*

the ten northern tribes, did pass out through the "gate" between the Black and Caspian Seas, breaking forth into the wilderness beyond. The following account of the beginning of their westward trek has been hidden from general view in the Apocrypha:

"Those are the ten tribes, which were carried away prisoners out of their own land in the time of Osea the king, whom Salmanasar the king of Assyria led away captive, and he carried them over the waters, and so came they into another land. But they took this counsel among themselves, that they would leave the multitude of the heathen, and go forth into a further country, where never mankind dwelt, that they might there keep their statutes, which they never kept in their own land. And they entered into Euphrates by the narrow passages of the river. For the most High then shewed signs for them, and held still the flood, till they were passed over. For through that country there was a great way to go, namely, of a year and a half: and the same region is called Arsareth." (II Esdras 13: 40-45.)

Jeremiah the Prophet was the instrument in God's hands to bring about the transfer of the House of David from the land of Palestine to the Isles in fulfillment of that part of his mission that had to do with "building and planting." The full commission was:

"See, I have this day set thee over the nations and over the kingdoms, to root out, and to pull down, and to destroy, and to throw down, to build, and to plant." (Jer. 1: 10.)

The phase of the prophet's mission that had to do with destruction was carried out in Palestine and in the messages he addressed to the surrounding nations. The second phase of his mission, *to build and to plant,* was carried out in a land far removed from Palestine. Because Jeremiah carried out the first part of his mission in detail, we

67

have every reason to believe that God saw to it that he fulfilled the second part as well. Jeremiah did not perish in the land of Egypt as some have contended, but lived to see the accomplishment of the whole task assigned to him. The evidence corroborating this statement is found in detail in the book entitled *Study in Jeremiah.**

The daughters of Zedekiah, the last king in Palestine to reign on the Throne of David, became Jeremiah's wards. Because God had promised that His covenant with David would never be broken, and that David would never lack a descendant to reign upon his throne ruling over the House of Israel, the royal line had to be preserved (see Jer. 33: 17). The task of transplanting the Seed Royal in the "appointed place" was, therefore, the "building and planting" phase of Jeremiah's commission. In Chapter 17 of *Study in Jeremiah* (pp. 279-299) this fascinating story is told. In the person of the king's daughter, together with the regalia of royalty taken by Jeremiah on his westward journey to the Isles, the Throne of David was literally transported from the "promised land" in the east to the "appointed place" north and west of Palestine.

THE LATTER DAYS

That royal planting became an accomplished fact long before the wandering peoples of the House of Israel arrived there. Actually, the ten tribes were breaking up into independent bands and beginning to move through the gateway of the Caucasus into the wilderness of Europe at the time Jeremiah was carrying out his mission. Centuries later, when the House of Israel began to be regathered in the Isles, they found their king already there before them.

* $3.50 postpaid. Destiny Publishers, Haverhill, Mass.

Hosea stated (Hosea 3: 5) that the House of Israel would fear the Lord and His goodness in the latter days; that is, during the Christian Dispensation. This is a direct indication that the people in the Isles, who became Christianized at the very outset of the Christian Era, were the House of Israel. It was only natural that they would respond to the Gospel, recognizing the attributes of their own God whose providence had preserved them and re-assembled them to become His people again through the redeeming love of His Son, Jesus Christ.

A Sinful Generation

Having now, for the third time, told of the coming captivity and ultimate deliverance and restoration of the House of Israel when, at the end of the years of chastening, they would again become God's people and He would be their God and a husband to them, Hosea was concerned next with the low spiritual condition of the people among whom he lived. He addressed a message to a sinful generation, demanding that they hear the word of the Lord:

"The Lord hath a controversy with the inhabitants of the land, because there is no truth, nor mercy, nor knowledge of God in the land." (Hosea 4: 1.)

Smith and Goodspeed translate this:

"The Lord has a quarrel with the inhabitants of the land; because there is no fidelity, no kindness, and no knowledge of God in the land."

These conditions were prevalent throughout the whole land of Israel just prior to the Assyrian invasion and deportation of the northern ten-tribed Kingdom, which began the long period of their captivity and chastisement.

Yet, the words of Hosea could just as readily apply to conditions extant throughout Anglo-Saxon lands today, for the House of Israel is again in the midst of a great apostasy. There is the same measure of lack of truth, mercy and knowledge of God in our land as that which existed in the time of Hosea. Crime today is on the increase; juvenile delinquency is a mounting menace, adding new recruits to the criminal element in the land.

Of far more serious proportions, however, is the extent to which a true knowledge of the Lord no longer exists in the nation. Spiritual understanding is at its lowest ebb. This latter condition is not being rectified by church services or attendance in Sunday School classes, for today very little actual instruction in the Word of the Lord is heard in the House of the Lord, with the result that the average Christian knows little or nothing about the Book of Life.

Hosea listed the results of the great apostasy of his time:

"By swearing, and lying, and killing, and stealing, and committing adultery, they break out, and blood toucheth blood." (Hosea 4: 2.)

Smith and Goodspeed render this:

"Cursing, lying, murder, theft, and adultery—They break out, and one crime follows hard upon another."

One needs only to read the daily accounts of crime to recognize how up-to-date Hosea's listing of the evils of his generation is, for the same evils plague our generation today. Actually the stream of swearing and cursing that rises from the lips of the people of the land exceeds in volume the prayers that ascend to God daily. Can God withhold judgment from a people who do such things?

Hosea warned his generation of impending judgment

and that judgment came. Jeremiah also warned his generation in similar terms when he said:

> "The land is full of adulterers; for because of swearing the land mourneth; the pleasant places of the wilderness are dried up, and their course is evil, and their force is not right." (Jer. 23: 10.)

The net result, Jeremiah declared, would be that God would bring evil upon them—"even the year of their visitation."

INDICATOR OF JUDGMENT

It is quite evident from the warnings of the prophets that, when the conditions described become the established pattern of life in a nation, the end of God's patience is reached and the next step is the descent of judgment. The steps in that judgment were indicated when Hosea described the adverse conditions to affect the land (Jeremiah states them to be drought, with the drying up of the wilderness). Hosea summarizes the result without referring specifically to the cause in this next statement:

> "Therefore shall the land mourn, and every one that dwelleth therein shall languish, with the beasts of the field, and with the fowls of heaven; yea, the fishes of the sea also shall be taken away." (Hosea 4: 3.)

It is the withholding of rain in due season that can and does bring about such changes as to compel even the fish of the sea to seek new feeding grounds. The altering of the rainfall alone produces climatic changes which greatly influence the habits of wild life upon the land and marine life in the waters of the earth.

In a very interesting little book titled *Today's Revolution in Weather* by William J. Baxter, the author points

71

out that weather changes now taking place throughout the world will have a direct effect upon business, health and all life upon this globe. There is an important factor involved here with which this book does not attempt to deal. This is the fact that the prophets of old tie in such changes with impending judgment, for they are a prelude to God's movements in retribution for gross wickedness among His people. In the preface to his book Mr. Baxter states in part:

> "Meteorologists frequently say that the weather averages out and that over a period of years there is not a great change in the average annual temperature. That does not mean a thing. Our studies show all over the world— whether we have studied Russia, Alaska, the Arctic Circle, New York City or London—the same phenomena, *that the heat zone is moving northward and the winters are getting milder with less snowfall."*

In easily understood terms and a highly readable style, the book presents a great deal of thought-provoking material concerning the revolution in weather now taking place throughout the earth. No one who reads the Bible can long remain unaware of the fact that the majority of the prophets vividly portray the tremendous changes in nature—of which the revolution in weather is merely the forerunner—which are the heralds of the ending of the age and the arrival of God's judgments in the earth.

FOREWARNINGS

When we read the accounts given by the prophets, repeating over and over again in detail the sins of God's people and the steps leading to inevitable judgment, it is not unnatural to question the reason why God has allowed so much space in the Scriptures to be devoted to this. The reason is quite clear. All this detail was provided, not only to give a definite example of inevitable judgment for evil, but in order that later generations may, by comparison, check the state of their own spirituality.

Thus, each succeeding generation can determine whether it has a right to claim Divine protection upon its undertakings or to expect nothing more than the visitation of judgment, of which impending troubles are but a prelude. When we peruse the accounts of the conditions outlined by the prophets which resulted in severe judgment coming upon the people of their generation, we have cause to be surprised and alarmed at the striking parallels between the evils of their day and ours.

Both Jeremiah and Hosea state that the evils of their times caused the withholding of rain in due season, the coming of drought and the resultant effect upon man and beast. It is of genuine interest to discover, disconcerting though it may be to those who will not heed the Divine admonition to turn from their unrighteous practices, that there is a definite pattern of changes so marked today in rainfall and climatic variations that they are being taken into account by scientists as they endeavor to determine the ultimate effect upon the present generation.

Hosea's warning to his generation, as well as Jeremiah's warning to the people of his day, could not be more timely when applied to our generation. The failure to heed the prophet's admonitions will see repeated in our generation as severe a degree of judgment as that which overwhelmed the people of Hosea's time. Through this prophet the Lord declared:

"My people are destroyed for lack of knowledge: because thou hast rejected knowledge, I will also reject thee, that thou shalt be no priest to me: seeing thou hast forgotten the law of thy God, I will also forget thy children." (Hosea 4: 6.)

REPUDIATED AS ADMINISTRATORS

"Thou shalt be no priest to me." This statement at once takes us back to the first mention of the word "priest" to the nation of Israel. When Israel was organized into the Kingdom of God at Mount Sinai, God gave them His commandments, statutes and judgments which they were to administer as the law of their land. The original statement made to Israel was:

"Now therefore, if ye will obey my voice indeed, and keep my covenant, then ye shall be a peculiar treasure unto me above all people: for all the earth is mine: And ye shall be unto me a kingdom of priests, and an holy nation." (Ex. 19: 5-6.)

Due to a lack of understanding of the national priestly functions in Israel, the use of the term "priest" requires clarification. The following paragraphs are quoted from *Primogenesis:*

"Unfortunately, the present meaning of the word 'priest' fails to adequately describe what was being proposed. Today, when speaking of priests, we think in terms of those who officiate at the altar in an ecclesiastical capacity. The Biblical definition of the priestly office is much broader in its application.

"It was the purpose and work of the Aaronic Order of priesthood to function ecclesiastically in the religious service of God's people. However, another order of priesthood, known as the Levitical Order, was also established in Israel and the priests of this order were not set apart for service in the Temple. On the contrary, they had charge of national affairs and from this priestly order the judges, lawyers, doctors, tax collectors and men in similar capacities were selected; in fact, the office of the Levitical Order was administrative and the priests of this order had charge of the affairs of God's Kingdom. It is of basic importance in understanding the story the Bible tells to always bear in mind the specific difference between the Aaronic and Levitical Orders of priesthood in the Israel Kingdom." (*Primogenesis*, p. 184.)

By their administration of the Law of the Lord in their land, Israel was to give the world an example of its perfection. The demonstration of peace and prosperity as the result of the operation of those laws in the Kingdom of God upon the earth was to be a marvel in the sight of all nations. Moses had declared to the people:

"Behold, I have taught you statutes and judgments, even as the Lord my God commanded me, that ye should do so in the land whither ye go to possess it. Keep therefore and do them; for this is your wisdom and your understanding in the sight of the nations, which shall hear all these statutes, and say, Surely this great nation is a wise and understanding people. For what nation is there so great, who hath God so nigh unto them, as the Lord our God is in all things that we call upon him for? And what nation is there so great, that hath statutes and judgments so righteous as all this law, which I set before you this day?" (Deut. 4: 5-8.)

But Israel failed miserably in carrying out God's great purpose which was to have been accomplished through them. The law had been given to guide and instruct them in righteousness. When they rejected the law, they rejected knowledge and it was for that reason that the Lord said through Hosea, "I will also reject thee, that thou shalt be no priest to me." Because of their rebellion against Him, God repudiated them as not fit to be the administrators of His law.

Continuing his indictment of his generation, Hosea

75

spoke of the failure of both prophets and priests and he did not exempt from condemnation the priests who officiated before the altar of the Lord. In similar terms Jeremiah condemned both prophets and priests in his time as profane men who were committing wickedness in the House of the Lord (Jer. 23: 11). Hosea stated that the glory that was once with those who functioned as prophets and priests among the people had turned to shame:

"Like people, like priest: and I will punish them for their ways, and reward them their doings. For they shall eat, and not have enough: they shall commit whoredom, and shall not increase: because they have left off to take heed to the Lord." (Hosea 4: 9-10.)

Instead of inquiring of the Lord for guidance, the people were asking counsel of their idols while they carried on the practices of their licentious worship. Judah was warned not to walk in the ways of Israel, for the Lord likened Israel to an obstinate, bucking heifer, refusing to be led as He would lead a lamb in pleasant pastures. Because of this, God said:

"Ephraim is joined to idols: let him alone." (Hosea 4: 17.)

This judgment was pronounced upon the head tribe of Ephraim, for the Ephraimites, the prophet said, were taking delight in the shame of their evil ways. In the simile of a furious wind enfolding them in its wings, their coming deportation was described, for the days of pleading with the House of Israel to repent and return to the Lord finally came to an end and God abandoned the people to the consequences of their own actions.

CHAPTER VI

A Great Apostasy

THE FIRST five chapters in this study of the Prophet Hosea, his life and utterances, cover the first four chapters of his book in the Bible. In his first two chapters, the prophet recounted the story of the rejection, punishment, regathering and ultimate restoration of the House of Israel in the last days. In his third chapter, Hosea pointed to impending judgment, followed by desolation, after which Israel would seek the Lord in the latter days. Then the great restoration would follow. In his fourth chapter, Hosea warned a sinful generation that an apostate people would not escape the wrath of God, but that punishment would certainly follow, and he outlined the severity of that punishment.

In the remainder of his book Hosea enlarged upon the details of his warnings as he pointed out the sins of priests, people and rulers of both Israel and Judah. The prophet contrasted the existing conditions in his day with those which had existed in earlier times. He condemned the outward show of repentance against the background of inward depravity and condemned the people for seeking alliances with foreigners, multiplying the extent of their revolt against God. He then warned that their moral failure would bring about political ruin and that their idolatrous practices and appeals to idols would not save them from destruction.

PRIESTS CONDEMNED

After having condemned Israel for their idolatry, which had resulted in a great apostasy in the land, Hosea then addressed a message to an apostate priesthood. He called upon Israel to take note and for the house of the king to give ear:

> "Hear ye this, O priests; and hearken, ye house of Israel; and give ye ear, O house of the king; for judgment is toward you, because ye have been a snare on Mizpah, and a net spread upon Tabor." (Hosea 5: 1.)

Contrary to generally-accepted teaching, Mizpah did not originally signify a benediction, but was, rather, a symbol of the necessity for watchfulness, keeping apart those who might pass over to harm one another (Gen. 31: 49). The name "Mizpah" means *watch tower* and Hosea was stating that the priests, who should have been watchmen upon the watch tower to warn God's people of impending danger, had become a snare to them by countenancing idolatry and allowing the people to be entangled as in a net spread to trap wild beasts. Hosea 5: 2, as translated by Smith and Goodspeed, describes the "revolters," or apostates, as having "dug deep the pit." Jesus referred to the spiritual leaders of His day in similar terms when He said:

> "Let them alone: they be blind leaders of the blind. And if the blind lead the blind, both shall fall into the ditch." (Matt. 15: 14.)

An interesting translation of Hosea 5: 2 by Delitzsch

shows to what a low state of spiritual degradation the priests of Hosea's time had fallen:

> "They understand from the very foundation how to spread out transgression."

PRAYERS UNHEARD

What the prophet declared the spiritual leaders of his day did to contribute to the general over-all apostasy of the time can be emphatically said of the religious leadership furnished by modernists who permeate Christian leadership in our churches today.

Hosea pointed to the misdeeds of the people, declaring they were not hid from God's sight. He emphasized that the evil they were doing prevented them from returning to God because of the apostate spirit within them. The prophet declared that Judah had also stumbled and, although both Judah and Israel might offer sacrifices, it would not now save them from their sins which had become so great that God would not hear their prayers. Because of the failure to keep the requirements of all His laws, Hosea declared that "they have begotten strange children."

STRANGE CHILDREN

The Hebrew word here translated "strange" is *zur*, which means an apostate or one given over to the idolatrous impurities of heathen religions. The prophet was referring to sons born in Israel who were practicing the evil abominations of the heathen. The fathers and mothers of this evil generation were condemned for their failure to properly bring up their offspring and teach them the precepts and laws of the Lord. The same evils of ungodliness, immorality and crime were rampant in Hosea's time that are widespread in our own time and the cause is the same—the failure to instruct each new generation in the ways of the Lord. The inevitable results were forecast by the prophet:

"Now shall a month devour them with their portions." (Hosea 5: 7.)

Ferrar Fenton translates the entire seventh verse as follows:

"The Lord you betrayed when you bore bastard sons,— Now a month will eat them and their herds."

By the expression, "a month," the prophet was indicating that in a very short time the complete disposal of these evil children would be accomplished.

BETRAYING THE LORD

The expression, "betraying the Lord," is of particular interest, for it means "to violate a trust" and "to deliver over to the enemy through faithlessness or treachery" that which belongs to the Lord. Parenthood in Israel carried with it the sacred trust of bringing up children in the knowledge and fear of the Lord. This was part of the covenant God made with His people:

"Now these are the commandments, the statutes, and the judgments, which the Lord your God commanded to teach you, that ye might do them in the land whither ye go to possess it: That thou mightest fear the Lord thy God, to keep all his statutes and his commandments, which I command thee, thou, and thy son, and thy son's son, all the days of thy life; and that thy days may be prolonged. Hear therefore, O Israel, and observe to do it; that it may be well with thee, and that ye may increase mightily, as the Lord God of thy fathers hath promised thee, in the land that floweth with milk and honey.

"Hear, O Israel: the Lord our God is one Lord: And thou shalt love the Lord thy God with all thine heart, and with all thy soul, and with all thy might. And these words, which I command thee this day, shall be in thine heart: And thou shalt teach them diligently unto thy children, and shalt talk of them when thou sittest in thine house, and when thou walkest by the way, and when thou liest down, and when thou risest up." (Deut. 6: 1-7.)

Hosea informed his generation that, by their failure to carry out these Divine injunctions, they had betrayed the Lord. Having been uninstructed in God's commandments, and having no faith and trust in their Lord, they had been rendered vulnerable to every Satanic influence. Actually they became a prey to the Arch Enemy of God for his exploitation and were therefore lost to the Kingdom and must be dealt with as strangers and not citizens of the Kingdom of God.

RESPONSIBILITY OF PARENTS

What was true in Hosea's time is equally true today and parents who fail to bring up their sons and daughters in the fear and knowledge of the Lord come under Divine condemnation. There is a tremendous responsibility placed upon parents in the sight of the Lord, who requires that they train their children to respect and obey His commandments. Failure to do so is to deal treacherously with the Lord.

When a generation comes into being in Israel that does not know God, judgment will not be long delayed as a, consequence. Hosea described the first phase of that judgment in terms of the punishment that overtook Benjamin for their sins. He selected Gibeah in Benjamin where the

Levite's concubine was mistreated by men of Benjamin, a crime which led to the slaughter of all of the tribe of Benjamin except three hundred men (see Judges, chapters 18-20).* The prophet exclaimed:

> "Blow ye the cornet in Gibeah, and the trumpet in Ramah: cry aloud at Beth-aven, after thee, O Benjamin." (Hosea 5: 8.)

House of Iniquity

Blowing the trumpet in Ramah, a city on the border of Benjamin, would signal invasion and war. The reference to Beth-aven was indicative of the state of apostasy in Israel, for Bethel means "House of God," while the meaning of Beth-aven is "house of naught" or "house of iniquity." Jeroboam profaned the place, or House, of God by establishing the worship of the golden calves there, for he had set one in Bethel and the other in Dan (I Kings 12: 29). Thus the House of God became the House of Iniquity.

Using Benjamin's sin and the subsequent almost complete annihilation of the tribe by the rest of Israel as an example, Hosea intimated that the first phase of destruction upon the children who had departed from the ways of the Lord would be slaughter from within. Benjamin was slaughtered by the rest of the tribes of Israel and the cry, "After thee, O Benjamin!" (that is, "the enemy is behind thee!") is a cry of war and refers to the time when, in the midst of battle, the men of Benjamin looked behind them and beheld their cities in flames. As a result they lost heart in continuing the battle and turned their backs on the foes in front, who then pursued and decisively

* See Chapter XXXVIII of *Primogenesis*.

defeated this tribe with a great slaughter (see Judges, chapter 20).

COMING DESOLATION

The next step in the process of judgment Hosea declared was to be desolation upon the tribes of Israel, which was pronounced in terms of punishment upon Ephraim, the headship tribe. But Judah was not to escape, for the prophet declared that their rulers were corrupt and practiced injustice. He likened their failure to deal righteously to one who removes ancient landmarks, a lawless act severely condemned under the Law of the Lord (Deut. 19: 14).

Hosea then depicted Ephraim as oppressed and broken in judgment because the House of Israel willfully followed the idolatrous practices of Jeroboam. The result was that the enemy invaded the land and made it a desolation in fulfillment of the curses that Moses said would come upon God's people when they turned away from His laws:

> "The fruit of thy land, and all thy labours, shall a nation which thou knowest not eat up; and thou shalt be only oppressed and crushed alway." (Deut. 28: 33.)

FORBIDDEN ALLIANCES

The prosperity of the people had vanished as the result of oppression and the invasions of the land by their enemies. Hosea gave them this message from the Lord:

> "Therefore will I be unto Ephraim as a moth, and to the house of Judah as rottenness." (Hosea 5: 12.)

The moth is a hidden destroyer and rottenness is caused by worms bred in decaying wood. This is indicative, therefore, of the kind of inward disintegration that was destroying His people. God likened Himself to destroying agencies of this type to demonstrate the inevitable outcome of the failure to obey His laws. Spiritual deterioration is inherent in disobedience to God's commandments and is the hidden factor bringing about complete moral and spiritual degeneration, just as the undiscovered moth destroys the uncared-for garment and undetected termites undermine and finally wreck the structure they infest.

The Septuagint version translates this verse:

"I will be like a terror to Ephraim, and like a goad to the house of Juda." (Hosea 5: 12.)

In spite of their suffering and troubles, the House of Israel refused to return to the Lord and instead turned for help to the Assyrians, sending Ambassadors to King Jareb. But the prophet declared there was no healing for Israel by this means, nor was her pain assuaged.

Jareb is thought by some to be an epithet applied by Hosea here and in Chapter 10: 6 to the King of Assyria. In a footnote in *The Companion Bible,* reference is made to Professor Sayce's book, *Higher Criticism and the Monuments* (pp. 416-417), where it is stated that Jareb may be the birth name of the usurper Sargon II, the successor of Shalmaneser. He points out that Shalmaneser did not take Samaria, but his successor did, as stated in an inscription found in the palace he built near Nineveh.

In conformity with God's covenant with them, His people had no right to seek alliances with the nations around them. The Lord had declared:

"Thou shalt make no covenant with them, nor with their gods." (Ex. 23: 32.)

Because Israel sought assistance from Assyria in her difficulties, the way was opened for this nation to become their oppressors, as pointed out in Ferrar Fenton's translation:

> "Then Ephraim went off to seek Ashur, and set loose the Ravaging King;—But he could not find you a cure, Nor could he take from you your sore!" (Hosea 5: 13.)

GOD BECOMES THE ADVERSARY

Actually the seeking of this alliance hastened the day when the enemy would invade the land of Israel in force. The Lord states as a result:

> "For I will be like a lion unto Ephraim, and like a young lion to the house of Judah. I will rend and be gone; I will carry off, with none to rescue. I will go back to my place, Until they realize their guilt, and seek my face; in their trouble they will seek me." (Hosea 5: 14-15, *Smith & Goodspeed Trans.*)

The Septuagint version translates this:

> "For I am like a panther to Ephraim, and like a lion to the house of Juda. When I tear, I will go and take and there shall be no deliverer. I will sally forth and return to my place until they are made desolate, then they will seek my face. In their affliction they will seek me early."

THE MODERN RAVAGER

In these three verses of less than sixty words Hosea covers the centuries of compulsion exerted upon His people under God's direction to compel them to seek Him. The sin of modern Israel is no different than that of our forefathers in Hosea's time. Then they made alliances with the Assyrians; today we are seeing the disastrous results of our covenants and agreements with the heathen rulers of Soviet Russia before, during and since World War II. Now this modern ravager, whom we have set loose, has grown powerful at our expense and he is moving forward unrelentingly toward the consummation of his goal—world domination.

The Lord declares that, as the result of their plight when they become helpless before the advance of the aggressor, His people will return to Him of their own volition. Throughout the centuries God has been waiting and now, as the age closes, the Israel nations are about to awaken to the real nature of their predicament under the pressure of an enemy seeking their annihilation. Hosea gives the timing of that awakening to spiritual values when, prophetically, he puts the following words into Israel's mouth:

"Come, and let us return unto the Lord: for he hath torn, and he will heal us; he hath smitten, and he will bind us up. After two days will he revive us: in the third day he will raise us up, and we shall live in his sight. Then shall we know, if we follow on to know the Lord: his going forth is prepared as the morning; and he shall come unto us as the rain, as the latter and former rain unto the earth." (Hosea 6: 1-3.)

AN APPEAL TO GOD

Joel confirms the fact that such a call will go out to God's people to return to Him, brought about as the result of the heathen nations gathering against them. He is more specific, even setting forth the type of prayer that will be uttered as the nation appeals to God for help:

"Gather the people, sanctify the congregation, assemble the elders, gather the children, and those that suck the breasts: let the bridegroom go forth of his chamber, and the bride out of her closet. Let the priests, the ministers of the Lord, weep between the porch and the altar, and let them say, Spare thy people, O Lord, and give not thine heritage to reproach, that the heathen should rule over them: wherefore should they say among the people, Where is their God?" (Joel 2: 16-17.)

THE ENEMY'S OBJECTIVE

Thus, as Hosea predicts, the people will, in the time of trouble, seek the Lord. It will indeed be a time of trial, for the enemy moving against the House of Israel is Gog of the land of Magog, the chief prince of Meshech (Moscow), at the head of a great confederacy, having as their objective the destruction of the House of Israel in the latter days (see Ezekiel, chapters 38 & 39). The present confederacy being consolidated under the leadership of Soviet Russia is fulfilling the predictions of Ezekiel's prophecy and will become the great army moving against God's people, causing them to pray the prayer given prophetically by Joel.

WEEK OF DAYS

The chronological timing of these developments is completely in step with Hosea's prediction and that of both Joel and Ezekiel, as well as other prophets. Hosea's statement, "After two days will he revive us," is worthy of close examination in the light of Peter's declaration:

"One day is with the Lord as a thousand years, and a thousand years as one day." (II Peter 3: 8.)

As pointed out in "The Fullness of the Ages," *Documentary Studies*, Vol. II, pages 57-70, in the great week of days, each day is one thousand years in length. Thus, three days had run their course from the beginning of human history, when Adam fell, to the dedication of the Temple at Jerusalem in 3000 A.M., or 1000-999 B.C. Three more days of 1000 years each remained from the dedication of the Temple to the great restoration and beginning of the millennial rule of our Lord.

During the one thousand years, or first day, following the dedication of the Temple, the House of Israel, and later the House of Judah, were carried into captivity. Israel was carried away to Assyria and Judah to Babylon. By the end of this day Jesus Christ was born (3996 A.M., or 4-3 B.C.). The second day, or thousand-year period, brought about the institution of His Church, with Israel in the Isles receiving the Gospel and the good news of their redemption being made known to them. The final one-thousand-year day, the third from the dedication of the Temple and the sixth from Adam in the great week of days (5000 A.M., or 1001-2 A.D., to 6000 A.M., or 2001-2 A.D.) began with the Norman Conquest when England was invaded by William the Conqueror and the Saxons were defeated in 1066 A.D. As pointed out in "The Fullness of the Ages":

"This is the last day of man's probation and before it ends the dispensation of the fullness of the ages will have become a fact as the Lord returns to take over His great authority and rule. This day is to end with the restitution of all things so that, when the millennial rest begins, perfection will have been established, while sin and trouble will pass away as righteousness is again restored to the earth. Just as man came into being at the end of the sixth day of creation, so, at the end of this sixth day of probation, the resurrection will occur and man, who lost the right to immortality because of sin, will receive this gift of God

88

through His Son, Jesus Christ." (*Documentary Studies,* Vol. II, p. 60.)

TWO AND THREE DAYS

Applying Hosea's two and three days to the history of Israel, beginning with the Israel-Syrian wars in 914-853 B.C., when Israel's power was greatly reduced, two days, or two thousand years, passed during which they were smitten and torn. Finally, under the pressure of adversity, they were driven westward. It was in the Eleventh Century that the Norman Conquest of England took place and the last of the tribes of Israel had gathered in the Isles. The period of revival prophesied by Hosea had begun. For the next few centuries, safely planted in their island home, the "appointed place" where Nathan the Prophet told David they would have rest from their enemies (II Sam. 7: 10), they began to renew their strength as Isaiah prophesied:

"Keep silence before me, O islands; and let the people renew their strength: let them come near; then let them speak: let us come near together to judgment." (Isa. 41: 1.)

EXPANSION OF MODERN ISRAEL

Hosea continued by saying, "In the third day he will raise us up, and we shall live in his sight." About the middle of the third day, a seven-times period (7 x 360) of two thousand years plus 520 years, or 2520 years, would be completed. This number of years after the Israel-Syrian wars saw the development of the Puritan Movement and responsible government in the British Isles. It also began the period of the expansion of the Anglo-Saxon peoples, the colonization of America and the growth of modern

Israel into the nation and the company of nations and great people of prophecy. Beginning with the Reformation in the midst of this third day, and the institution of missionary activities at the outset of the Nineteenth Century, Isaiah's prophecy began to be fulfilled. Drawing near to the Lord, the people began to speak in His name as they carried the Gospel of Salvation to the ends of the earth.

Before they will be able to draw together to the Lord in judgment, however, modern Israel must awaken to the knowledge of their origin and identity so that they may arise to their responsibilities. This is the meaning of the invitation by Hosea, "Let us return." But it will be only the recognition of the superior power of an almost-victorious enemy moving against God's people that will compel them to realize and acknowledge that they are the Israel of God, as so clearly set forth by Joel. Then the fulfillment of Jeremiah's prophecy will come about:

> "All they that devour thee shall be devoured; and all thine adversaries, every one of them, shall go into captivity; and they that spoil thee shall be a spoil, and all that prey upon thee will I give for a prey. For I will restore health unto thee, and I will heal thee of thy wounds, saith the Lord." (Jer. 30: 16-17.)

LIVING IN GOD'S SIGHT

This healing will come, according to Hosea, when "He will raise us up, and we shall live in his sight." This will bring about the fulfillment of Isaiah's words:

> "Arise, shine; for thy light is come, and the glory of the Lord is risen upon thee." (Isa. 60: 1.)

No wonder Hosea exclaims, "Then shall we know!" All

of our present troubles stem from a lack of knowledge of the Lord and the failure to recognize the necessity to keep His laws. If, then, as intimated by the prophet, we follow on to know the Lord, we shall live in His sight. This is the awakening of Israel to newness of life, fulfilling Ezekiel's prediction of a great spiritual awakening as set forth in the 36th and 37th chapters of his book.

Hosea then declares of the Lord:

"His going forth is prepared as the morning; and he shall come unto us as the rain, as the latter and former rain unto the earth." (Hosea 6: 3.)

TIME OF RESTORATION

There is nothing that can be substituted for refreshing rain to restore life, fertility and productiveness to the parched earth. By his use of this simile, the prophet is referring here to the only remedy that will restore His people in righteousness and bring renewal of life to His Kingdom—the return of Jesus Christ! It is He who will accomplish the complete discomfiture of His enemies and the enemies of His Kingdom. Joel shows this close association of judgment and renewal:

"I will remove far off from you the northern army, and will drive him into a land barren and desolate. . . . Fear not, O land; be glad and rejoice: for the Lord will do great things. . . . Be glad then, ye children of Zion, and rejoice in the Lord your God: for he hath given you the former rain moderately, and he will cause to come down for you the rain, the former rain, and the latter rain in the first month." (Joel 2: 20-23.)

This will result, according to Joel, in the full restoration of prosperity to His people, for they will then know

that the Lord is among them. Never again will there be
any need for His people to be ashamed for, as stated by
Peter in Acts 3: 19, "The times of refreshing shall come
from the presence of the Lord."

CHAPTER VII

Transgressing the Covenant

EVEN IN Hosea's time there were those who were aware of the significance of what the prophet was saying and their counsel was, "Come and let us return unto the Lord." While this invitation had an interesting prophetic fulfillment as pointed out in the previous chapter, yet in Hosea's time it was expressed by those who were greatly concerned because of the apostasy in Israel. However, this desire of the few who understood the purport of Hosea's warnings was not generally heeded, as evidenced by what followed.

PIETY LACKING

God's appraisal of the spiritual condition of the people was an answer to those who urged their countrymen to repent and return to the Lord:

> "What shall I do with you, O Ephraim? What shall I do with you, O Judah? For your piety is like a morning cloud, or like the dew that leaves early." (Hosea 6: 4, *Smith & Goodspeed Trans.*)

There was such a complete lack of spiritual depth among the people and their worship of God was so superficial that He described their piety as like the passing of a morning cloud or like the dew that disappears with the rising of the sun. There was no true spiritual longing back of the suggested return to the Lord, but only a desire to escape the results of disobedience.

INCREASED PRESSURE

Because His people were insincere in their attitude toward Him, the Lord declared:

> "Therefore will I hew them by the prophets; I will slay them by the words of my mouth, and my judgment will go forth like the light. For I delight in piety, not sacrifice; and in the knowledge of God, rather than burnt-offerings." (Hosea 6: 5-6, *Smith & Goodspeed Trans.*)

From the beginning, in God's dealings with His people as a nation, He has found it necessary to send prophets to warn them against disobeying His will, pointing out that the troubles they encounter are the results that follow when they ignore Him. Throughout the ages His people have been hewn; that is, cut and shaped under the pressure of judgment, correcting the teachable and slaying (*i.e.,* utterly condemning to destruction) the incorrigible by the words of His mouth. The statement that the Lord delights in piety rather than in sacrifice is His condemnation of much that has been done by men and women in their endeavor to merit His approval, engaging in the ritual of sacrifices and personal affliction as a substitute for righteousness and personal purity.

KNOWLEDGE OF GOD ESSENTIAL

High on the list of that which is acceptable in the sight of the Lord is the acquisition of a full knowledge of His commandments, statutes and judgments. The lack of this alone is responsible for much of the failure on the part of

94

God's people to do all that He requires of them. Hundreds of thousands of Christians are so ignorant of God's plans and purposes today that the Bible, His Written Word, has become a closed book to them. Hosea shows that such an understanding of the Lord is declared to be far more essential than the offering of burnt sacrifices. In modern times this would include the observance of religious ritualisms. Even this, although rendered in the name of the Lord, cannot be accepted as a substitute for a practical understanding of His Word that results in a life lived in conformity with His laws.

BREAKING THE COVENANT

It is a self-evident fact that when evil practices become predominant in the daily conduct of the people, the contributing cause is an abject ignorance of what the Divine law requires. What inevitably follows is a direct transgression of God's covenant with His people, a fact Hosea confirms:

"But they like men have transgressed the covenant: there have they dealt treacherously against me." (Hosea 6: 7.)

Ferrar Fenton renders this:

"But like Adam you broke from the contract. You always were faithless to Me!"

This was a reference to the covenant God made with Israel at Mount Sinai when the people became His kingdom upon earth. He was warning them that the judgment about to descend upon them was due directly to their failure to keep the terms of this national covenant. They were ignoring His precepts and failing to obey His laws. As a consequence, they found it easy to take up idolatrous practices and the worship of the gods of the nations around them. God saw that this turning away from Him was deliberate on the part of His people, for He referred to their transgression as like that of Adam, who partook of the forbidden fruit, knowing what the consequences would be.

CITIES OF REFUGE

Ramoth-Gilead was one of the cities of refuge (Joshua 21: 38) to which those accused of the crime of killing another could flee for protection. In the 35th chapter of Numbers the operation of the law in regard to cities of refuge is given in detail. It was in Ramoth-Gilead that a person involved in a crime which included the death of another person was judged and if he was proved innocent of murder, he was allowed to remain in the city for protection from the avenger of blood; that is, the one charged with the responsibility of executing the criminal guilty of murder. Those involved in cases of accidental death could find protection in these cities and upon the death of the High Priest they were set free.

There is more than one reason why the accused person was compelled to remain in the city of refuge to which he had fled until the death of the High Priest. In the first place the life of each individual is sacred in the eyes of the Lord and the Law of the Lord provides for its full protection. No man can take life with impunity, whether premeditated or accidental. His sin is not only against the commandment, "Thou shalt not kill," but it is a crime according to the law of his nation and a sin against his generation. Therefore, he was not free from judgment until the death of the High Priest, for the bounds of the generation in which he was found guilty were set by the days of the life of the High Priest who had jurisdiction.

There is another, and more important, factor to consider here as well. In the old dispensation the High Priest prefigured the coming of Jesus Christ, who has become our High Priest after the Order of Melchisedec (Heb. 6: 20). He stood, therefore, as the mediator between the accused man and his God. At the death of the High Priest the man was released, just as every sinner before God is released from judgment under the law when he comes in repentance to Jesus Christ who is our High Priest in this Christian Dispensation.

A CORRUPT PRIESTHOOD

In Hosea's time, however, the city of refuge, Ramoth-Gilead, had become utterly corrupt:

> "Gilead is a city of them that work iniquity, and is polluted with blood. And as troops of robbers wait for a man, so the company of priests murder in the way by consent: for they commit lewdness [enormity]." (Hosea 6: 8-9.)

Justice was no longer obtainable in this city. The priests who were charged with administering the law were actually profiting by murder, evidently using the necessity for protection of those who fled to the city as a means to extort money from them in the form of bribes. Thus the Divine denunciation of these priests was that they were like troops of robbers laying in wait for a man. Perhaps, when their demands were not met, they turned the refugee over to the avenger of blood; therefore, the accusation against them was that they murdered "in the way by consent." Because they practiced vice instead of rendering just judgment, God condemned those who should have judged righteously to be judged themselves according to their own unrighteousness. When it is considered that the

97

High Priest was ordained to be the representative of Christ, it is realized how deplorable the conditions in Ramoth-Gilead were.

TIME OF HARVEST

Referring to the idolatrous practices of the people and their worship of the Golden Calf at Bethel, with all the accompanying evil and licentiousness of the adopted pagan rituals, the Lord declared through Hosea:

> "In Bethel, I saw a horrible thing; there Ephraim played the harlot, Israel was defiled. For you too, O Judah, a harvest is appointed." (Hosea 6: 10-11, *Smith & Goodspeed Trans.*)

Here Hosea refers to the fact that the harvest time for his generation had come and Judah is specifically mentioned as approaching her harvest, as well as Israel. Moral and spiritual degeneration had reached the low degree among the people where only the impending judgment could halt the rampant evil in their midst.

INTERNAL CORRUPTION

Hosea asserted that, when God would have healed His people, the guilt of Ephraim was discovered and the sin of Samaria was made known, although the people seemed to be completely unmindful of the fact that nothing is hid from the eyes of the Lord:

> "They have wrought falsehood, and the thief comes in; gangs prowl about. But they never realize that I shall remember all their wickedness." (Hosea 7: 1-2, *Smith & Goodspeed Trans.*)

While this was an indictment of Hosea's generation, it could as readily apply to conditions today due to the corruption in our midst. Crimes of all kinds are on the increase; robberies and murders are frequent occurrences; gangs of hoodlums prowl about, committing acts of vandalism. Daily news reports reveal the shocking practices of groups of teenagers in search of excitement. Juvenile delinquency is the contributing cause of this degeneracy and this is the result of the failure to bring the precepts of the Word of the Lord to the attention of the young people of the land.

It was pointed out in the preceding chapter that God condemns the parents of the children who have departed from him, declaring that they betray him when they do not bring up their children in the knowledge and fear of the Lord. God is thwarted in His desire to restore past blessings to His people, for their wickedness and the deeds of violence from border to border witness against them:

> For thieves are within;—robbers pillage outside! Nor reflect in their heart I remember their crimes, tho' they wrap up their acts, from My face!" (Hosea 7: 1-2, *Ferrar Fenton Trans.*)

Hosea maintained that even the kings of Israel were undismayed by existing conditions, for the revenue derived from evil practices was pleasing to them. Hosea then pointed to the evils resulting from drinking themselves into a state of intoxication and the unrighteous revelries that followed, stating that the king and the princes had corrupted themselves, as well as the people. Hosea declared they readily committed murder while inflamed with wine, killing their magistrates one after another.

These wretched conditions were the inevitable outcome of generations of falling away from the Lord. The continual lowering of the spiritual standards of the people could only result eventually in a low caliber of leadership, for out from among spiritually bankrupt people come spiritually depraved rulers. The results are always as Hosea described them. There was no one left to call upon the Lord to ask for deliverance from the internal evils which were causing the breakdown of the whole structure of national well-being.

DECLINE OF EPHRAIM

When we consider that Great Britain represents modern Ephraim in the world today, Hosea's remarks take on a very significant prophetic meaning:

"Ephraim wastes away among the peoples; Ephraim is a cake unturned. Strangers devour his strength, without his knowledge; gray hairs are scattered upon him, without his knowledge. And the pride of Israel witnesses against him; But they do not return to the Lord, their God, nor seek him for all this." (Hosea 7: 8-10, *Smith & Goodspeed Trans.*)

This is a remarkable prophetic description of the calamities which have overtaken modern Ephraim today. We are hearing it proclaimed in many quarters that Great Britain has lost much of her former standing as a great empire; that she is wasting away as her colonial possessions are taken from her one after another. Foreigners are devouring her strength and her colonial possessions are falling into the hands of those who are strangers to the justice and equity of Israel's laws. The actions of Nehru in India and Naguib and his successors in Egypt are examples of the fulfillment of these prophetic statements in our time.

One of the sources of the strength of the Israel nations was the possession of the "gates" of their enemies (Gen.

24: 60). Chief among these is the Suez Canal. Now this, as well as other strategic "gates" (Gibraltar, Cyprus, etc.) are being claimed by other nations and Ephraim finds herself with little strength left to hold on to them. Ferrar Fenton renders Hosea 7: 9 as follows:

> "Strangers suck out his [Ephraim's] strength, and he knows not! He has sprinkled grey hairs, but he never perceives!"

Hosea goes on, "And the pride of Israel witnesses against him." In a note in *The Companion Bible* it is stated that "the pride of Israel" is "an appellation of Jehovah." In other words, it is the Lord in whom Israel should have gloried and found her strength. Instead of this, Hosea pointed out that the people would not return to the Lord, nor seek His help. Therefore, as the Ferrar Fenton rendering shows, Ephraim does not perceive that the loss of her strength is due to her failure to repent and restore the righteousness of the Law of the Lord in her land and then call upon the Lord to undertake for her in her hour of weakness.

FOREIGN ALLIANCES CONDEMNED

The outcome of the lamentable failure in leadership is Hosea's condemnation:

> "For Ephraim has become like a silly dove, without sense; they call to Egypt, they go to Assyria." (Hosea 7: 11, *Smith & Goodspeed Trans.*)

If we substitute "Soviet Russia" and "Communist China" for "Egypt" and "Assyria," we observe a striking parallel between the seeking of foreign alliances in Hosea's day and the quest for such alliances in modern times! This, Hosea declares, is the reason why their strength is depleted and he exclaims that "Ephraim is as a cake unturned!" In modern colloquialism the phrase would be: "half-baked."

In the eyes of all Ephraim is aging, but Hosea says that, although the "grey hairs" have appeared, he is not aware of this. And, indeed, the appearance of gray hairs need not impair the strength of the man who fears and serves God and relies implicitly upon Him for guidance. It was said of Moses at the end of his career as a leader in Israel:

"And Moses was an hundred and twenty years old when he died: his eye was not dim, nor his natural force abated." (Deut. 34: 7.)

This is stirring testimony in behalf of a man who revered and served his God and honored and obeyed His laws all the days of his life.

The seeking of foreign alliances by God's people is definitely forbidden, the Lord having cautioned Israel regarding the nations around them:

"Thou shalt make no covenant with them, nor with their gods. They shall not dwell in thy land, lest they make thee sin against me: for if thou serve their gods, it will surely be a snare unto thee." (Ex. 23: 32-33.)

When Israel persisted in entering into covenants with the nations around them, Hosea warned them the Lord had declared that, if they followed such a course, He would be in opposition to them:

"When they shall go, I will spread my net upon them; I will bring them down as the fowls of the heaven; I will chastise them, as their congregation hath heard." (Hosea 7: 12.)

This allusion to "their congregation" is a reference to Moses' prophecies read in the hearing of all the people, *i.e.,* the *congregation* of Israel. In those prophecies Moses was instructed by the Lord to set before Israel two ways in which they might go—one the way of life and blessing and the other the way of death and cursing. If the people obeyed the Lord and kept all His commandments, statutes and judgments, wonderful blessings, with national prosperity, would follow. But if they refused, then troubles would afflict them and Moses listed the curses that would overtake them (see Leviticus, chapter 26, and Deuteronomy, chapter 28).

Hosea was referring to the curses pronounced by Moses as about to come upon his generation because of the disobedience of the people and their refusal to keep the terms of God's covenant with them so that He would be able to bless them. Through Hosea the Lord declared:

> "Woe to them! wanderers from Me!
> Alas for them! who revolted from Me!
> When I rescued, about Me they lied!
> They called not to Me from their hearts,
> Altho' they have yelled on their beds!
> They assemble for corn and for wine,
>   But rebel against Me!"
>   (Hosea 7: 13-14, *Ferrar Fenton Trans.*)

Smith and Goodspeed translate the 14th verse as follows:

> "They do not cry unto me from their hearts, but wail upon their couches for grain and wine; They cut themselves and rebel against me."

COMPOUNDED REBELLION

Involved in God's controversy with Israel was His own honor, for it was well known among the Gentiles and the heathen that He had promised to bless His people. They could not appreciate the fact, of course, that He was prevented from doing so by the sins of His own people, for His stipulation had been that He would not bless them while they disobeyed His laws. Their attempts to give lip service to Him were an abomination in His sight because He knew the insincerity of their hearts. When trouble came they were willing to look to the Lord for deliverance and their descendants in Anglo-Saxondom in these modern times have repeated their superficial supplications in days of prayer for peace throughout two world wars and in the face of the third. The Lord continued His complaint:

> "If I weakened or strengthened their arms, Yet they thought but of mischief for Me! They do not rebound,— they are like worthless bows; So their Princes shall fall by the sword, because of their swaggering tongues; They are scorned in the country of Mitzer [Egypt]." (Hosea 7: 15-16, *Ferrar Fenton Trans.*)

All this came to pass when Israel was forced to go into Assyrian captivity and while this message is primarily addressed by Hosea to the people of his generation, it is also a prophetic message addressed to the generation of God's people living in the time of the ending of the present age. Due to the seriousness of these times, and because God has broken the power of His people, reducing them to a state of impotency as they face the gathering storm of turmoil and war, they have become the scorn of the heathen around them. Today this is evidenced in the attitude of the Asiatics as they press forward in their aggressions without regard to Anglo-Saxon opposition.

DESTRUCTION COMING

Hosea was instructed to announce the coming of judgment by means of the sound of a trumpet. This was to be the signal that the destroying "eagle" (vulture) was moving against God's people:

"Set the trumpet to thy mouth. He shall come as an eagle against the house of the Lord, because they have transgressed my covenant, and trespassed against my law." (Hosea 8: 1.)

Through Hosea God declared that when the enemy comes against them:

"Israel shall cry unto me, My God, we know thee." (Hosea 8: 2.)

But the prophet exclaimed:

"Israel hath cast off the thing that is good: the enemy shall pursue him." (Hosea 8: 3.)

Having refused to choose the course that would have enabled God to move to save them, they could no longer stand before their enemies. Neither was God able to come to their assistance while they continued in their sins, so their appeal to Him for help in a time of crisis brought Hosea's declaration, "the enemy shall pursue them."

Hosea gave a list of additional reasons for this judgment, stating that the people had set up kings and princes, but not men selected by God. He declared that their silver and gold had been made into idols. The prophet pronounced judgment upon the calf they worshipped, declaring it was to be broken into pieces. Then he exclaimed:

"For they have sown the wind, and they shall reap the whirlwind." (Hosea 8: 7.)

In reference to economic conditions throughout the land, the Lord stated that their standing grain which had no sprout would yield no meal. What little yield there was would be devoured by foreigners.

ISRAEL SWALLOWED UP

The next pronouncement by the Lord graphically depicts what happened to the House of Israel as the result of their captivity and dispersion among the Gentiles:

"Israel is swallowed up: now shall they be among the Gentiles as a vessel wherein is no pleasure." (Hosea 8: 8.)

Smith and Goodspeed render this:

"Israel shall be devoured; Soon shall they be among the nations like a worthless thing."

In II Kings 17: 6-23 we have the historical record of the swallowing up of Israel as predicted by Hosea. Words could not more plainly state what happened to the people. The House of Israel disappeared from sight and from history for many generations and it was during this period that the people became "lost." It was not until the nineteenth and twentieth centuries that their identity began to be recognized again. Today the Anglo-Saxon-Celtic peoples stand forth as those who bear every one of the many marks by which the prophets have stated the House of Israel was to once more become known in the latter days.

FINAL ACT OF REBELLION

Prior to the time the armies of Assyria actually moved to attack Israel, alliances had been made with the nations around them and this, Hosea declared, completed their rebellion against God. The prophet referred to it as the final move on their part that would result in their being carried away into a foreign land:

"For they have gone up to Assyria, like a wild ass wandering by itself; Ephraim gives love-gifts. But though they hire among the nations, I will soon gather them up; and they shall cease a while from anointing a king and princes." (Hosea 8: 9-10, *Smith & Goodspeed Trans.*)

A wild ass is stubborn and wilful and will not be guided or curbed. Equally so, Ephraim ignored the word of the Lord and tried to form unnatural alliances with nations which were their traditional enemies. The reference to going up to Assyria refers to the seeking of such an alliance with this nation. They hoped in doing so to maintain their independence, wilfully ignoring what they knew to be true, that only in turning to the Lord could they hope to continue as a nation free from enemy domination. The nation whom they sought to appease turned out to be a deadly foe that brought their nation down to ruin.

It is of interest to note that the Smith and Goodspeed rendering of Hosea 8: 10, "and they shall cease a while from anointing a king and princes," is very similar to Hosea's earlier prophecy:

"For the children of Israel shall abide many days without a king, and without a prince." (Hosea 3: 4.)

This came to pass during the many years of wandering when the tribes escaped from their Assyrian captors and dwelt in the wilderness, then trekked through the land of Europe, eventually arriving in the isles north and west of Palestine where they were to renew their strength (Isa. 41: 1). Hosea also prophesied:

"Afterward shall the children of Israel return, and seek the Lord their God, and David their king; and shall fear the Lord and his goodness in the latter days." (Hosea 3: 5.)

This is a prophetic reference to the ultimate restoration

of Israel to favor with God. But before it takes place, their wilful pride and stubbornness must be replaced by a spirit of humility and repentance. They must come to the place where they are willing to learn the important lesson that Hosea's record of the past actions of their forefathers is able to teach. The nations of Anglo-Saxondom must cease entering into agreements and pacts with nations who repudiate their God, lest their action be regarded by the Lord as a final act of rebellion against Him on their part that will bring about the day of swift retribution. When His people learn to fear the Lord and obey His commandments, they will experience the full measure of His goodness in their behalf as the age ends and a new order of righteousness is ushered in.

CHAPTER VIII

The Departing Glory

UNDER THE LEADERSHIP of the birthright tribe of Ephraim, the House of Israel held God's laws in contempt, considering them of little value. They were no longer emulating the righteousness of their forefathers and God refused to recognize their demonstrations of piety. Because of the increase and enormity of their sins, the prophet announced that final judgment would soon overtake the people:

> "Now will he [God] remember their iniquity, and visit their sins: they shall return to Egypt. For Israel hath forgotten his Maker." (Hosea 8: 13-14.)

RETURN TO BONDAGE

The statement, "they shall return to Egypt," typified their coming bondage in Assyrian captivity. Actually it should have been a warning of more ominous portent to them than a direct threat that they would become subject to Assyria, for they were undoubtedly well acquainted with the history of the cruel bondage of their forefathers in Egypt. When finally the House of Israel was taken into Assyrian captivity, it is true that some fled to Egypt. But there was no escape for them there, for they found only graves for themselves in that land.

Because Israel had forgotten their Maker, they built idolatrous temples and palaces. On the other hand Judah, refusing to trust the Lord for their safety, built fortified cities. Hosea declared that the fire of God's anger would burn these temples and palaces and destroy the fenced cities.

Israel was severely reproved for ascribing their prosperity to idols when they rejoiced at harvest time in the great plenty received from their threshing floors. The prophet declared they would face famine, for the prosperity for which they no longer thanked God was to cease. They would not be allowed to continue to dwell in the Lord's land. Again it was stated that they would "return to Egypt"; that is, to bondage. They would begin to eat unclean things—*i.e.,* foods forbidden in the Law of the Lord—in the land of Assyria (Hosea 9: 3). Meantime, the pleasant places where they had been living would become a desolation.

CERTAINTY OF JUDGMENT

Evidently it was under the pressure of adverse criticism against his prophecies that Hosea asserted:

"The days of punishment will come; The days of requital will come; Israel shall know." (Hosea 9: 7, *Smith & Goodspeed Trans.*)

What is it that Israel was to know? One truth they would come to understand was that the prophets in their midst who foretold peace and plenty were fools. They would eventually realize that those who claimed to be inspired, but who were not led of the Spirit of the Lord, were mad, for all their counsel would come to nought. But the prophets whom Hosea called watchmen among them, who were warning of trouble to come, were of God because they remained faithful to their calling uninfluenced by public clamor for words of peace when they knew there would be no peace.

Turning his attention to the false prophets, Hosea likened their prognostications to the snare of a fowler, for they had corrupted themselves with crimes similar to those that caused most of the tribe of Benjamin to be destroyed, as set forth in the Book of Judges (chapters 19-21). These prophets, therefore, were moral degenerates. Under this debased leadership Hosea pointed to the impure rituals the people performed in worshiping Baalpeor. What made matters even worse, they loved to have it so.

Love Turned to Hatred

God had formerly loved them but the prophet declared that, because of their wickedness, His love had now turned to hatred of their evil ways. Therefore God loved them no more. They were soon to cease being God's Kingdom people, for He was willing to cast them away into Assyrian captivity. Because they refused to heed the prophet's warning to turn from their evil ways, they were to become wanderers among the nations (Hosea 9: 17).

Likening Israel to an empty vine that has cast its grapes, Hosea pictured the fruitlessness of the nation. He declared they were ruined by their prosperity because they attempted to serve both God and Mammon; i.e., both Jehovah and Baal, with the result that God had rejected them as His people. Nevertheless, He would see to it that their altars were broken down and their images destroyed. To the people of Israel in such a time of prosperity it would seem that these predictions could not be fulfilled and the words of the prophet would be very unpopular among them. It is easy to see why Hosea was thoroughly disliked.

OATH BREAKERS

Yet there was at that time no stable government in the land, administering the law in righteousness. The cynical attitude of the people toward their rulers is portrayed by their words:

"For they will soon be saying, 'We have no king; for we do not revere the Lord; and as for that, what could the king do for us?' They speak mere words; they swear false oaths; they make leagues; and judgment will blossom forth, like weeds in the furrows of the field." (Hosea 10: 3-4, *Smith & Goodspeed Trans.*)

Israel's kings had been making alliances contrary to God's covenant with the people. Also, in making these forbidden agreements, they had sworn falsely, for they had no intention of keeping faith with those with whom they had made leagues. The Lord declared they would be put to shame for such perfidy.

According to the standard of righteousness which they are expected to uphold, even when Israel makes forbidden alliances, they must keep their word, even though it proves to be to their own detriment. The outstanding example of this in Israel's history was the alliance Joshua and the elders of Israel made with the Gibeonites (Joshua, 9th chapter). Because of their refusal to abide by the requirements of the Law of the Lord, Hosea declared the king of Samaria would be cut off "as the foam upon the water" (Hosea 10: 7).

A Call to Repentance

Nevertheless, all hope for deliverance for the people was not completely lost. Speaking in terms of husbandry, the prophet pleaded with Israel:

"Sow to yourselves in righteousness, reap in mercy; break up your fallow ground: for it is time to seek the Lord, till he come and rain righteousness upon you." (Hosea 10: 12.)

Hosea was calling upon the people to "break up the fallow ground"; that is, turn from their stubborn and evil ways so that the seeds of truth and justice might enter into their hearts and bear fruit. Speaking to them in the same analogous terms, he pointed out what they had been doing:

"Ye have plowed wickedness, ye have reaped iniquity; ye have eaten the fruit of lies: because thou didst trust in thy way, in the multitude of thy mighty men." (Hosea 10: 13.)

Inadequacy of Military Might

Hosea reminded them that if they refused to heed the call to seek the Lord and persisted in trusting in their prosperity and military strength, the outcome would be disastrous:

"Therefore shall a tumult arise among thy people, and all thy fortresses shall be spoiled." (Hosea 10: 14.)

Their military might and their strong places of defense would not save them if they continued their idolatrous practices. They would be completely routed by their foes with sudden finality, for Hosea prophesied, "In a morning shall the king of Israel utterly be cut off"

(Hosea 10: 15). This prediction became a reality when Samaria was captured by the Assyrians and the people were carried away into captivity.

CALLED OUT OF EGYPT

Contrasting Israel's early faith with the great apostasy in evidence in Hosea's time, the prophet again harked back to the experiences of their forefathers in Egypt, but this time to remind the people of God's love for them:

"When Israel was a child, then I loved him, and called my son out of Egypt." (Hosea 11: 1.)

While this reference is to the call of Israel out of Egypt under Moses, it was also prophetic of a later event when Mary and Joseph, with the young child Jesus, the Son of God, had fled into Egypt:

"And was there until the death of Herod: that it might be fulfilled which was spoken of the Lord by the prophet, saying, Out of Egypt have I called my son." (Matt. 2: 15.)

Here is the remarkable mingling of the historical calling of Israel out of Egypt with a prophecy of the calling of the Son of God out of the land of Egypt also, to be fulfilled at a later time. The blending of the literal and the prophetic, as the Bible deals with the history of Israel and the events pertaining to Him who is to become King and reign over the House of Jacob forever, demonstrates the wonderful, guiding power of the Holy Spirit demonstrated in the words chosen by the prophets to express facts of history which are themselves also prophetic of future facts.

Unable to Forsake

Because Israel had descended further and further into the evil depths of idolatry, the more Hosea called upon them to turn back to the Lord, the more perverse and disobedient they became. Instead of listening to the words of the prophet and obeying their God, they turned more and more to their idols. Although it was God who had tenderly cared for His people, teaching and guiding them, taking hold of their arm as one would teach a child to walk, supporting them through all their difficulties, yet they refused to acknowledge His goodness.

Once more a reference is made to Egypt, but here the inference is that the people might think of Egypt as typifying a peaceful escape since it was in the land of Goshen that their forefathers lived in prosperity and security:

"He shall not return into the land of Egypt, but the Assyrian shall be his king, because they refused to return [*i.e.,* to Jehovah]." (Hosea 11: 5.)

The people were being warned that when the Assyrian became their king, there would be no place of peace and plenty (Goshen) in the land of their captivity. The repeated references to Egypt are most interesting, indicative as they are of the fact that undoubtedly the people were in this way reminded many times of how difficult their existence would be in Gentile bondage in an effort to persuade them to repent and return to the Lord.

In the former experience the descent into Egypt was permitted by the Lord to preserve the lives of His people in a time of famine and He made it possible for them to dwell in the land of Goshen. Perhaps the people sarcastically reminded Hosea that life in Goshen was very good. But this time their bondage in Assyrian captivity would be wholly punitive, with no relief from cruel slavery anywhere in the land.

Nevertheless, Hosea provides a glimpse of the anguish of God's heart because the gross sins of His people compelled Him to punish them severely. Their iniquity was so great that there was no reason why they should not be utterly destroyed. Yet the Lord exclaimed:

"How shall I give thee up, Ephraim? How shall I deliver thee, Israel? How shall I make thee as Admah? How shall I set thee as Zeboim? Mine heart is turned within me, my repentings are kindled together." (Hosea 11: 8.)

Because God could not consent to the annihilation of His people, as Admah and Zeboim (kings associated with the kings of Sodom and Gomorrah) had been routed and slain in an earlier time, His words were:

"I will not execute the fierceness of mine anger, I will not return to destroy Ephraim: for I am God, and not man; the Holy One in the midst of thee: and I will not enter into the city." (Hosea 11: 9.)

This statement, "I will not enter into the city," alludes to the entry of the two angels into Sodom, heralding the final condemnation of the city and its inhabitants to utter destruction because the cup of its iniquity was full (Gen. 19: 1-13). God was here declaring that He would deliberately refrain from entering into the cities of the House of Israel as a testimony against them, for had He done so, the people could not have escaped complete annihilation.

For the Elect's Sake

Because God cannot look upon sin with any degree of tolerance whatever (Hab. 1: 13), He must move in judgment against all who violate His laws. The alternatives for Israel in Hosea's time were repentance or judgment. If God had "entered into their cities," however, this would have constituted a judicial act of finality on His part as their Judge, preindicating the inevitability of judgment that would have ended in total destruction, for their sins merited the death penalty. But, as Hosea records, God refused to move among them as their Judge.

What is the position of the nations of the House of Israel today in relation to Divine justice? The modern disobedience to God's laws and repudiation of Divine commandments is bringing judgment upon the world as violence, bloodshed and war sweep over the earth. But just as God did not enter into the cities of Israel to destroy His people then, so now He is planning to move to prevent the cup of iniquity of His people from running over, making their annihilation inevitable. Jesus explained that the restraining power of Divine intervention in our time, shortening the days of tribulation lest all flesh be destroyed, would be only for the sake of the elect:

> "And except those days should be shortened, there shall no flesh be saved: but for the elect's sake those days shall be shortened." (Matt. 24: 22.)

We are now living in the time designated as "those days" and every reason is present why the verdict of annihilation should be rendered against a civilization that ignores God. It is only the presence of the elect of

117

God who have stayed the Divine hand so that the clock of the ages may be stopped short of the hour of execution of final, irrevocable judgment.

WHEN THE LION ROARS

Looking forward from Hosea's day, the Lord promised a time to come when Israel would be compelled to return to Him. Hosea was inspired to declare:

"They shall walk after the Lord: he shall roar like a lion: when he shall roar, then the children shall tremble from the west." (Hosea 11: 10.)

Here is a unique prophecy of the coming of the Lion of the Tribe of Judah—Jesus Christ. It should be noticed particularly that the choice of titles used is a specific indication of the time of fulfillment of this prophecy. It was the Lord's coming as their Redeemer that would bring about the restoration of His people to Himself, delivering them from their divorced condition. But His coming as the Roaring Lion can refer only to the Time of His triumphant return and the full import of this is outlined in detail in the chapter, "The Roaring Lion," in *Documentary Studies*, Vol. III, Part VII (pp. 283-291).

CHILDREN IN WEST

The prophecy states that when the Lion roars, the "children in the west" shall tremble. Those called "children" here will be the descendants of those whom Hosea was condemning for their evil ways and they will then be residing in the West. It is interesting to recall that Jesus was mindful of the need to send the glad tidings of His coming as Redeemer to the outcast House of Israel. Therefore, He instructed His disciples not to go into the way of the Gentiles:

"But go rather to the lost sheep of the house of Israel."
(Matt. 10: 6.)

History now reveals that it was to Israel regathered in
the Isles north and west of Palestine that the Gospel was
taken after our Lord's crucifixion, resurrection from the
dead and ascension. There He was proclaimed as their
Redeemer and Saviour and they were exhorted to accept
Him and bring their lives into conformity with His commandments.

These "children in the west" will tremble when they
behold Him roaring as the Lion of Judah, triumphantly
returning as King of kings and Lord of lords, for they
will not be spiritually ready to receive Him. But they will
be compelled by the pressure of judgment to repent of
their sins, renounce their iniquitous practices and, as
Hosea foretold, "They shall walk after the Lord."

RULING WITH GOD

In the final verse of the 11th chapter Hosea again took
up his task of reporting the sins of God's people in his
day. Here, as a matter of fact, we have the divisions of
authority among His people at that time clearly pointed
out:

> "Ephraim compasseth me about with lies, and the house
> of Israel with deceit: but Judah yet ruleth with God, and
> is faithful with the saints." (Hosea 11: 12.)

The leadership of the House of Israel was vested in the
tribe of Ephraim, which held the birthright. Therefore,
Ephraim was specifically named in the condemnation of
the House of Israel for their gross sins. The House of
Israel was at the point of being divorced from God, but
the House of Judah had not yet forfeited their position

of ruling with God. The capital of Judah was still at Jerusalem, where kings of the House of David reigned upon the Throne of the Lord. The Temple was also there, enabling the people to be faithful in their worship of the Lord. The word "saint" used here is simply a term applying to Israel as God's people, for they were selected and set apart to become a servant people dedicated to the holy purpose of making the Divine laws and will known throughout the earth.*

An East Wind

The recounting of the Lord's quarrel with Ephraim, the headship tribe of the House of Israel, was continued and those in power in Samaria were accused of following the "east wind" (Hosea 12: 1). In eastern countries an East wind is evidence of wasting and desolation and a parched earth. Actually Ephraim was attempting to make covenants with the Assyrians and sending oil into Egypt. But the Lord, through Hosea, was derisively pointing out that the Egyptians would abandon them in their time of distress and the Assyrians would become their oppressors.

The Call to Return

But Judah soon began to turn away from the Lord, for Hosea announced that God's controversy was with them as well as with Israel. The Prophet Jeremiah recorded the Lord's judgment upon this defection as he witnessed it:

> "And I saw, when for all the causes whereby backsliding Israel committed adultery I had put her away, and given her a bill of divorce; yet her treacherous sister Judah feared not, but went and played the harlot also." (Jer. 3: 8.)

* See *Documentary Studies,* Vol. I, p. 391.

Using the unconverted name of "Jacob" to apply to all
Israel, the Lord reminded His people of His dealings with
their father Jacob, how he had prevailed over Esau and
had talked with God at Bethel. It is stated that Jacob
found his Lord at Bethel, a significant term denoting that
the Lord became his God from that day forward and was
with him all the rest of his life. The prophet then addressed Israel:

> "Therefore turn thou to thy God: keep mercy and judg-
> ment and wait on thy God continually." (Hosea 12: 6.)

FALSE WEIGHTS AND MEASURES

Through the prophet God put His finger, so to speak,
on one of the base sins of His people:

> "He is a merchant, the balances of deceit are in his hand:
> he loveth to oppress." (Hosea 12: 7.)

Honesty in business transactions was to be a basic
virtue among the Lord's people and they were condemned
for violating the law which states:

> "Thou shalt not have in thy bag divers weights, a great
> and a small. Thou shalt not have in thine house divers
> measures, a great and a small. But thou shalt have a perfect
> and just weight, a perfect and just measure shalt thou
> have. . . . For all that do such things, and all that do
> unrighteously, are an abomination unto the Lord." (Deut.
> 25: 13-16.)

Completely ignoring this standard of righteousness,
Israel was boasting of their gains regardless of the unjust
manner in which their wealth was being acquired. Their
attitude was that God was prospering them, so what they
were doing could not be as sinful as the prophet described
it to be (Hosea 12: 8). Such an attitude is often assumed

by those who do evil when the retribution which is expected to be the result does not immediately manifest itself. Success in the acquiring of wealth, they reason, justifies the means used, thus making the successful accumulation of wealth itself the criterion of right.

Again Become Wanderers

Through Hosea the people were reminded that from the time of their deliverance from the land of Egypt, the Lord had been their God. He had sent His prophets to them to exhort them to repent and restore righteousness, but they refused to pay any attention to them. Therefore the Lord threatened through Hosea that He would reduce the people to poverty and cause them to again become wanderers, no longer dwelling in houses but in tents (Hosea 12: 9). Events from the early life of their forefather Jacob were recounted to them, showing how God had nurtured them from humble beginnings. Then Hosea pointed out that it was by a prophet (Moses) that they were delivered from Egypt and by the same prophet they were preserved in their wilderness wanderings (Hosea 12: 13). Now Ephraim and the House of Israel had provoked the Lord to bitter anger because of their great wickedness, as Ferrar Fenton translates Hosea 12: 15:

"For he is all spattered with bloodshed!—So his Judge will fix infamy on him!"

When Ephraim was meek and humble, he became great in God's sight, but the sentence of death had been pronounced upon that greatness because the people and their leaders had turned to idolatry (Hosea 13: 1). A reference was made to their having kissed the idols (calves) and this indicated to what extent they had succumbed to idolatry

(Hosea 13: 2). To kiss an idol or other venerated object was considered an act of most solemn adoration.

Therefore, the passing of their greatness would be like the morning cloud that drifts swiftly away and the early dew that soon dries up. Also, their worth among the nations would be like the chaff driven before the wind and the smoke that goes up the chimney (Hosea 13: 3). The Lord promised He would make them understand they would not go unpunished when they gave credit to heathen idols for what He had done for them:

"Yet I am the Lord thy God from the land of Egypt, and thou shalt know no god but me: for there is no saviour beside me." (Hosea 13: 4.)

Only Source of Deliverance

Speaking in terms of a lion or leopard lying to wait for their prey, the Lord indicated the suddenness of the destruction that would shortly overtake His people. The ferocity of the attack and the suffering to follow was likened to that of the victim of the anger of a bear bereaved of her whelps. God then fixed the question of guilt, but He mercifully did not fail to mention the one source from which they could hope for deliverance:

"O Israel, thou hast destroyed thyself; but in me is thine help. I will be thy king: where is any other that may save thee in all thy cities?" (Hosea 13: 9-10.)

God had given them a king in the first place in compliance with their shortsighted request, even though it angered Him that they preferred an earthly king to Himself as their Ruler. Then, in His wrath because of their sinfulness, He took their king away. But in this statement the Lord makes a promise that He will again be Israel's king and this will be fulfilled in the coming of Him who will be King of kings and Lord of lords.

Meanwhile, however, because the iniquity of Ephraim had been registered in the Divine court of justice and the indictment was ready (Hosea 13: 12), the Lord spoke in strange terms concerning the fate of His people (Hosea 13: 13). The analogy of childbirth is used and reference is made to the crisis in parturition if, due to lack of strength or other hindrance, the infant does not come forth and is strangled in birth. This example typified the disaster which overtook the Kingdom of God in Hosea's day.

The purpose of the Kingdom was to administer the Law of the Lord, set an example of blessing for all the nations to see and eventually (as Daniel later prophesied) fill the whole earth with righteousness. Hosea was undoubtedly well aware of Isaiah's prophecy that the Kingdom of God was to be exalted above all governments and "all nations shall flow unto it" (Isa. 2: 2-3). Yet, in the very inception of the fulfillment of this glorious mission, and before the influence and domain of the Kingdom had been able to spread beyond the confines of the land of its birth, the people refused to exert the moral strength to survive. Therefore, their strangulation as a nation in Assyrian captivity was inevitable and the spiritual power and greatness which might have been theirs died a-borning when they were driven from the land of Palestine.

CHAPTER IX

Ransomed from the Grave

THE GREAT THEME running throughout the Scriptures, first mentioned in the Pentateuch and culminating in the Book of Revelation, is the symbolic relationship of husband and wife existing between the Lord God Jehovah and His people Israel. That this was so from their inception as the nation chosen to become the nucleus of the Kingdom of God on earth is made clear by the Prophet Jeremiah. He records the words of the Lord which refer to the day He "took Israel by the hand" to lead them out of the land of Egypt. At that time, the Lord stated, "I was an husband unto them" (Jer. 31: 32).

It has already been shown in Chapter II that when the House of Israel turned away from God to embrace gross idolatry, He repudiated them as His people, designating them as an unfaithful wife. God declared He would no longer be a husband to them and gave the House of Israel (not Judah) a bill of divorcement and "put them away" out of their own land. They were, therefore, unable to escape defeat by the invading Assyrian armies and were carried away into Assyrian captivity.

ASSYRIAN GRAVEYARD

Describing the subsequent circumstances of the House of Israel, Hosea used an analogous term of great and far-reaching significance. He likened their captivity in Assyria to a graveyard (Hosea 13: 14) and this depicts more accurately than any other mode of expression what actually occurred. It is because of what occurs in death that the deportation of the House of Israel into Assyria was so fittingly compared to the descent into the grave. The grave is a place of forgetfulness as Solomon declared:

"There is no work, nor device, nor knowledge, nor wisdom, in the grave, whither thou goest." (Ecc. 9: 10.)

To this the Psalmist added:

"For in death there is no remembrance of thee." (Ps. 6: 5.)

Therefore, in the grave there is neither *knowledge* nor *memory*.* How aptly this describes what happened to the House of Israel. The people soon lost all contact with their former activities and surroundings and before long all knowledge and remembrance of their origin and identity dimmed and vanished away. After an interval of time there is scarcely anything less identifiable than an unmarked grave and this was equally true of the people who had once been known as a prosperous kingdom protected by the might of their powerful God and who had inhabited a land given to them by Divine right.

DEATH-LAND

In his translation of the Scriptures, Dr. James Moffatt provides a very interesting version of Hosea's reference

* See *Documentary Studies,* Vol. III, Part X.

to death and the grave in connection with Israel's captivity. In the form of questions, the Lord's words are interpreted as asking:

> "Am I to save them from Death-land? Am I to rescue them from death?" (Hosea 13: 14.)

This rendering positively identifies Assyria as the death-*land* into which Israel was to be flung for their sins. The emphasis upon the fact that a "land" is involved is firm support of the conclusion that the land of Assyria was to be to the House of Israel a spiritual graveyard.

REDEEMING ISRAEL

Nevertheless, the account of God's dealings with His people does not end here. While it is true that in the grave of Assyrian captivity Israel ceased to remember former things and lost all knowledge of their past, they were not to remain there for all time, nor be divorced from God forever. But before it would be possible for them to again live in God's sight, there must be a resurrection from this grave of forgetfulness. Just as the individual is impotent to implement his own deliverance from the grave, so, too, the House of Israel was helpless to bring about their own restoration. Therefore, through Hosea the Lord declared He would be their Redeemer and Deliverer:

> "I will ransom them from the power of the grave; I will redeem them from death." (Hosea 13: 14.)

It has already been shown in earlier chapters that it was Jesus Christ, the Son of God, who was later to pay the ransom in behalf of His people with His own life on the cross of Calvary. As their Redeemer, Jesus Christ alone could deliver the House of Israel from the power of the grave and raise them up so that they might live again in God's sight.

Quoting the words of the Lord, Hosea assures us there will be no change in the Divine purpose to redeem Israel from death. The certainty of this is expressed in the statement, "Repentance shall be hid from mine eyes"; that is, there will be no change of mind on the part of God, dissuading Him from His ultimate objective—the redemption of His people. This statement follows the challenging declaration:

"O death, I will be thy plagues; O grave, I will be thy destruction." (Hosea 13: 14.)

A NATIONAL RESURRECTION

In the extremely important 15th chapter of I Corinthians, familiarly known as the "resurrection chapter" of the New Testament, Paul undoubtedly had Hosea's prophecy in mind when he triumphantly exclaimed:

"Death is swallowed up in victory. O death, where is thy sting? O grave, where is thy victory?" (I Cor. 15: 54-55.)

Throughout this chapter Paul discoursed at length concerning the nature and purpose of the resurrection and Christians are indebted to him for much detailed information concerning what they may anticipate as individuals when this phenomena becomes a reality in experience.* However, the primary application of the declaration by Hosea, which inspired Paul's statement, was to typify the method by which the redemption of the House of Israel from their Assyrian grave would be accomplished.

* See "Each In His Own Order," *Documentary Studies*, Vol. II, pp. 639-651.

VALLEY OF DRY BONES

The Prophet Ezekiel was shown a remarkable vision of Israel in her grave:

"The hand of the Lord was upon me, and carried me out in the spirit of the Lord, and set me down in the midst of the valley which was full of bones, and caused me to pass by them round about: and, behold, there were very many in the open valley; and, lo, they were very dry.

"And he said unto me, son of man, can these bones live? And I answered, O Lord God, thou knowest. Again he said unto me, Prophesy upon these bones, and say unto them, O ye dry bones, hear the word of the Lord. Thus saith the Lord God unto these bones; Behold, I will cause breath to enter into you, and ye shall live: And I will lay sinews upon you, and will bring up flesh upon you, and cover you with skin, and put breath in you, and ye shall live; and ye shall know that I am the Lord.

"So I prophesied as I was commanded: and as I prophesied, there was a noise, and behold a shaking, and the bones came together, bone to his bone. And when I beheld, lo, the sinews and the flesh came up upon them, and the skin covered them above: but there was no breath in them. Then said he unto me, Prophesy unto the wind, prophesy, son of man, and say to the wind, Thus saith the Lord God; Come from the four winds, O breath, and breathe upon these slain, that they may live. So I prophesied as he commanded me, and the breath came into them, and they lived, and stood up upon their feet, an exceeding great army." (Ez. 37: 1-10.)

That these dry bones represented the House of Israel in their apparently helpless state in the grave of forgetfulness was definitely stated when the vision was explained to the prophet:

WHOLE MEANS BOTH HOUSE, The HOUSE OF ISRAEL
WITH THE HOUSE OF JUDAH. AURTHOR IS WRONG
HERE!

STUDY IN HOSEA

"Son of man, these bones are the whole house of Israel [therefore, they represented the people who had been taken captive into Assyria]: behold, they say, Our bones are dried, and our hope is lost: we are cut off for our parts." (Ez. 37: 11.)

Smith & Goodspeed render this:

"O mortal man, these bones are the whole house of Israel. Behold, they keep saying, 'Our bones are dried up, and our hope is lost; we are completely cut off.'"

The identification of the "dry bones" with the House of Israel could not be more pointedly clear and the words put into the mouths of the people were indicative of their hopeless condition. They were cut off from God by divorce and unable to regain the blessing lost because of the curse of the law which separated them from God.

Even after they had left the land of Assyria, Ezekiel's vision still depicts them figuratively as dry bones scattered far and wide over a great valley. Therefore they remained dormant, still in a state of death; they continued to be separated from their land, their king and their temple (Hosea 3: 4). As time went on they became scattered throughout the "wilderness of the people" (Ez. 20: 35) and among the heathen (Ps. 44: 11). Their movements through history were shrouded in silence, but Esdras gives us a glimpse of them as they commenced their westward trek:

"Those are the ten tribes, which were carried away prisoners out of their own land in the time of Osea [Hosea] the king, whom Salmanasar, the king of Assyria, led away captive, and he carried them over the waters, and so came they into another land. But they took this counsel among themselves, that they would leave the multitude of the heathen, and go forth into a further country, where never mankind dwelt. That they might there keep their statutes, which they never kept in their own land. And they entered into Euphrates by the narrow passages of the river. For the most High then shewed signs for them, and held still the flood, till they were passed over. For through that country there was a great way to go, namely, of a year and a half: and the same region is called Arsareth. Then dwelt they there until the latter time." (II Esdras 13: 40-46.)

THE WORD OF THE LORD

Ezekiel was told to address a message from the Lord to the dry bones of the House of Israel:

"O ye dry bones, hear the word of the Lord." (Ez. 37: 4.)

When the Nation of the Jews would not accept Jesus Christ as their Messiah, He pronounced the sentence upon them that they would lose the custodianship of the Kingdom of God:

"The kingdom of God shall be taken from you, and given to a nation bringing forth the fruits thereof." (Matt. 21: 43.)

Ezekiel's prophecy that the "valley of dry bones" was to hear the word of the Lord began to be fulfilled when Jesus informed the Jews that, because they had rejected Him, their house would be left unto them desolate (Matt. 23: 38). The nation to which Jesus referred which would receive the Kingdom was the House of Israel, for Jesus had already given instructions to His disciples to go to them and proclaim the Gospel of the Kingdom to them:

"These twelve Jesus sent forth, and commanded them, saying, Go not into the way of the Gentiles, and into any city of the Samaritans enter ye not: But go rather to the lost sheep of the house of Israel. And as ye go, preach, saying, The kingdom of heaven is at hand." (Matt. 10: 5-7.)

131

Isaiah gave a marvelous prophecy of the coming birth of a child who would be called Wonderful, Counsellor, the Mighty God, the Everlasting Father, the Prince of Peace. He stated that the government would be upon His shoulder and that there would be no end to its expansion and peace because this would be accomplished "upon the throne of David, and upon his kingdom" (Isa. 9: 6-7). After this the significant statement was made:

"The Lord sent a word into Jacob, and it hath lighted upon Israel. And all the people shall know, even Ephraim and the inhabitant of Samaria." (Isa. 9: 8-9.)

Ephraim Israel—that is, the House of Israel—the people who had inhabited Samaria, typified by Ezekiel's vision as dry bones filling a great valley, were to hear the word of the Lord. Isaiah declares the Word was sent "into Jacob," a fact confirmed by John who announced that, in the birth of Jesus Christ, the Word was made flesh (John 1: 14). John's statement that the Jews refused to receive Him (John 1: 11) complemented Isaiah's prophecy that the Word, leaving them, would light upon Israel.

GRACE IN THE WILDERNESS

The Prophet Jeremiah also supports this fact in his prophecies, showing that, having left the land of their Assyrian captors and while dwelling in the wilderness, Israel would find grace there:

"Thus saith the Lord, The people which were left of the sword found grace in the wilderness; even Israel, when I went to cause him to rest." (Jer. 31: 2.)

Jeremiah was led to prophesy that a time would come (in the latter days) when the Lord would again be "the God of all the families of Israel" (Jer. 31: 1), but before this could occur, His people must find grace through their Saviour. Following the crucifixion and resurrection of Jesus Christ, the Word was taken to Israel, for persecution in Jerusalem and throughout Judea and Galilee drove many of the converts to Christianity to seek refuge with Israel in northern lands and dwelling in the "isles of the sea"—the British Isles.

This is all graphically described by Ezekiel who, in his vision, heard the noise of a great shaking when bone came to bone and this was followed by sinews, flesh and skin covering the bodies of the "slain." The prophet was beholding a scene that prefigured the gradual process of the spiritual awakening that began while Israel trekked through the wilderness and has extended down through the centuries. From the time that our Lord's disciples began to carry the glad tidings of their redemption to the House of Israel to the present day, the continuing task has been to make known to the nations of Israel—the Anglo-Saxon-Celtic peoples—the fact that they have been ransomed from the grave and may again become recovenanted to God as His people by the grace of Jesus Christ. But their complete resurrection and restoration to God's favor has not as yet taken place.

An Exceeding Great Army

In the meantime, however, as Hosea prophesied, the number of the descendants of the House of Israel has become "as the sand of the sea, which cannot be measured nor numbered" (Hosea 1: 10). They are, as Ezekiel envisioned, standing on their feet, "an exceeding great army" (Ez. 37: 10), for today the world beholds them as the company of nations of the British Commonwealth of Nations and the great people of the United States of America

(Gen. 48: 19), together with kindred peoples and nations. God stated through the Prophet Amos what He would do:

> "For, lo, I will command, and I will sift the house of Israel among all nations, like as corn is sifted in a sieve, yet shall not the least grain fall upon the earth [to be lost sight of or unaccounted for]." (Amos 9: 9.)

Now that they have been gathered together again as nations, they are being severely disciplined in preparation for the day when God will pour out His Spirit upon them.

CHAPTER X

Life from the Dead

WHEN THE TIME CAME for the Prophet Hosea to conclude his prophetic messages to the House of Israel, he looked forward in vision to future generations of the people and beheld them under forlorn circumstances, still separated from their God. Knowing that, in spite of their sinfulness, they were not beyond Divine help, he issued the call:

"O Israel, return unto the Lord thy God; for thou hast fallen by thine iniquity." (Hosea 14: 1.)

These words were addressed to a people who had suffered much because of their disobedience of the commandments, statutes and judgments of the Lord, and would have still more to suffer if they did not repent. The prophet proceeds to instruct the people in the proper approach to God, counseling them to carefully choose the words they are to use when they return to Him so that their restoration may be permanent. "Take with you words," the prophet says, "and turn to the Lord" (Hosea 14: 2). Then he gives the prayer Israel is to pray in the latter days, just before their final deliverance:

"Take away all iniquity, and receive us graciously: so will we render the calves of our lips. Asshur shall not save us; we will not ride upon horses: neither will we say any more to the work of our hands, Ye are our gods: for in thee the fatherless findeth mercy." (Hosea 14: 2-3.)

PRAYER FOR DELIVERANCE

The first step is to humbly beseech the Lord to take away the iniquity of His people. In a footnote in *The Companion Bible* it is pointed out that the word "graciously" may be more properly rendered, "O Gracious One." *The Companion Bible* states further that certain eminent Jewish commentators took this as a title of the Messiah. This would give emphasis to the fact that this prayer can only be prayed in the latter days, after the appearance of Jesus Christ as Redeemer and Saviour.

In the next phrase of the prayer, "so will we render the calves of our lips," the words "calves" and "lips" are metonyms, to be understood as figuratively suggesting that which they do not actually express. The reference is to the calves offered in sacrifice and the Lord repeatedly condemned His people in former days for carrying out the form and ritual of sacrifice while their hearts were far from Him. Thus, the prayer of the people is to be couched in sincere words; the "sacrifices of their lips" are to be heartfelt words of praise, thanksgiving and gratitude, coupled with their promise to be truly obedient. This is another way of saying what is expressed in the 50th Psalm:

"Offer unto God thanksgiving; and pay thy vows unto the most High: and call upon me in the day of trouble; I will deliver thee, and thou shalt glorify me." (Ps. 50: 14-15.)

Following this there is to be a specific repudiation of the three aspects of defection which led directly to Israel's captivity. They are to say: "Asshur shall not save us." It was their association with the Gentile nations around

136

them, entering into leagues and agreements with them, that caused Israel to sin, for they violated the commandment:

"Thou shalt make no covenant with them, nor with their gods." (Ex. 23: 32.)

Then they are to say: "We will not ride upon horses." This was a reference to the proud Egyptian cavalry and was an allusion to Israel's propensity to run to Egypt for help, instead of appealing to the Lord, when their enemies threatened them with invasion.

Finally they are to say: "Neither will we say any more to the works of our hands, Ye are our gods." There is to be an utter repudiation of all types of idolatry, including Israel's stubborn refusal to accept the Lord's judgment, as expressed in His Word, as better than their own and willingly obey His commandments. That stubbornness is a form of idolatry was plainly stated when King Saul became rebellious and only partially carried out the Lord's edict concerning the Amalekites (I Sam. 15: 23).

Smith and Goodspeed translate Hosea 14: 1-3 as follows:

"Return, O Israel, to the Lord, your God; For you have stumbled in your guilt. Take with you words, and return to the Lord. Say to him, 'Wholly forgive guilt; and we will take what is good, and requite thee with the fruits of our lips. Assyria shall not deliver us; Nor will we ride upon war-horses; Nor will we say any longer, "Our God," to the work of our own hands; for in thee the orphan finds mercy.' "

Ferrar Fenton renders Israel's penitent prayer:

"Say, 'Removing our errors, have mercy,
For we offer the fruits of our lips;—

For Ashur shall not be our Saviour,—
And on horses no more will we ride,—
No more will we call those our gods,
That we, ourselves, made by our hands;
Only You for the orphaned have pity.' "

The reference here to the "orphaned" is of special interest, for Hosea's message is addressed to the "orphaned children" (descendants) of the divorced "mother" (Israel) who had been put away by her Divine Husband.

ANSWER TO PRAYER

The Prophet Joel outlines the prayer the nations of Israel are to pray so that they may be delivered from their enemies (Joel 2: 17). Hosea, on the other hand, gives the petition to be prayed by God's people when they sincerely repent and express their desire to be fully restored to covenant relationship with their God again.

Joel records in detail the answer God will make and the action He is prepared to take in behalf of His people when the specific prayer is prayed according to the instructions given (Joel 2: 18-27). Equally so, Hosea records the Lord's gracious promise, to be fulfilled when His people turn to Him in prayer as Scripturally directed and beseech Him to be reinstated in His favor:

"I will heal their backsliding, I will love them freely: for mine anger is turned away from him. I will be as the dew unto Israel: he shall grow as the lily, and cast forth his roots as Lebanon. His branches shall spread, and his beauty shall be as the olive tree, and his smell as Lebanon." (Hosea 14: 4-6.)

WHEN THE PRODIGAL RETURNS

Couched in the figurative terms of a parable, Jesus gave a prophecy of the return of the House of Israel to God

(Luke 15: 11-32). He said that "a certain man" had "two sons" and one went into a "far country" while the other remained at home. The "man" was God, the Father; the "son" who remained at home was the House of Judah (not divorced); the "son" who went into the far country was the House of Israel, becoming Lo-ammi, *i.e.*, "not God's people" (Hosea 1: 9). Having this understanding of the characters in the story, the plot becomes clear. The analogy depicts Israel as coming to himself and returning, to be greeted with open arms by the Lord who is ready and waiting to pour out abundant blessings upon His genuinely repentant people.

Israel's Fall

The Apostle Paul speaks of Israel's separation from God through divorcement as a "fall." But he emphasizes the fact that their restoration to favor with God will have a far greater impact upon the world than the benefits which accrued to the Gentiles because God was compelled to find a way to redeem His people and thus wrought salvation for all mankind. Speaking of the blindness of Israel the apostle says:

> "Do I therefore say, 'They have stumbled, so that they might fall?' Never! But that by their mistake the salvation has come to the heathen, so as to arouse themselves. But if their mistake enriches the world, and their loss is wealth for nations, how much more will their prosperity be! . . . For if their dispersion reunites a world, what will their reunion be but life from the dead?" (Rom. 11: 11-15, *Ferrar Fenton Trans.*)

The Divine Redeemer

It was only by death that the stipulations of the law of divorcement which separated God from His people could

139

be wiped out (Deut. 24: 1-4). God moved, therefore, to provide redemption from this law for His people and its accomplishment was committed into the hands of His only begotten Son, Jesus Christ, who became the Testator of a new and better covenant (Heb. 9: 14-17). When Jesus Christ became the Redeemer of Israel, He made it possible for God's people to be recovenanted to Him under the New Covenant. This provided for the fulfillment of what was previsioned in Hosea 1: 10. It also made it possible for the ultimate symbolism of the Divine remarriage to take place (Rev. 19: 7).

At the same time, however, Jesus became the Saviour of mankind as well as of His people so that all, regardless of race, who will believe and accept Him, may be saved and receive eternal life. This is why Paul said that it was because of Israel's mistake that salvation had come to the Gentiles and the heathen (Rom. 11: 32). Nevertheless, the apostle asserted that, marvelous as all this was, when Israel finally becomes reconciled to God, it will be a far greater happening. In fact, the effect upon the world will be as startling and electrifying as though the dead had come to life! The King James Version renders the 15th verse of Romans 11 as follows:

"For if the casting away of them be the reconciling of the world, what shall the receiving of them be, but life from the dead?"

Smith and Goodspeed translate this:

"For if their rejection has meant the reconciling of the world, what can the acceptance of them mean but life from the dead?"

This statement of Paul's is far more than a mere figure of speech. Actually the dead are to be involved when the

Kingdom of God is restored in full perfection. This is made quite clear from Scriptural passages which show that, by means of a resurrection from among the dead— the First Resurrection—those will come forth who are to be associated with the Lord in the government of the restored Kingdom.

THEN SHALL THEY KNOW

Coupled with this, and no less real in its accomplishment as an actual fact, is the restoration from "death" of the House of Israel whom Ezekiel depicts as resurrected from the "grave of forgetfulness" upon the command of the Lord:

> "Thus saith the Lord God; Behold, O my people, I will open your graves, and cause you to come up out of your graves, and bring you into the land of Israel. And ye shall know that I am the Lord, when I have opened your graves, O my people, and brought you up out of your graves, and shall put my spirit in you, and ye shall live, and I shall place you in your own land: then shall ye know that I the Lord have spoken it, and performed it, saith the Lord." (Ez. 37: 12-14.)

Prerequisite to this great spiritual reawakening among the nations of modern Israel, when the Lord will put His Spirit into the hearts of the people, is their recognition and acknowledgment of their identity when, "as life from the dead," they will be revealed to themselves and to all nations as His people. This revelation is closely associated with the time when God moves to save them from their enemies, causing the hordes of Gog of the land of Magog to meet with overwhelming defeat. Ezekiel declares of that time:

> "And all the heathen shall see my judgment that I have

executed, and my hand that I have laid upon them. So the house of Israel shall know that I am the Lord their God from that day and forward. And the heathen shall know that the house of Israel went into captivity for their iniquity. . . . When I have brought them again from the people, and gathered them out of their enemies' lands, and am sanctified in that them in the sight of many nations; Then shall they know that I am the Lord their God, which caused them to be led into captivity among the heathen. . . . Neither will I hide my face any more from them: for I have poured out my spirit upon the house of Israel, saith the Lord God." (Ez. 39: 21-29.)

THE TRIUMPHANT REMNANT

The seventh verse of Hosea's final chapter opens with a qualifying phrase to which special attention should be given:

"They that dwell under his shadow shall return; they shall revive as the corn, and grow as the vine: the scent thereof shall be as the wine of Lebanon." (Hosea 14: 7.)

This immediately brings to mind the opening verse of the 91st Psalm:

"He that dwelleth in the secret place of the most High shall abide under the shadow of the Almighty." (Ps. 91: 1.)

It is of interest, too, to note that the *Targum*, referring to those who "dwell under his shadow," makes this statement:

"They shall be gathered together from the midst of their captivity; they shall dwell under the shadow of *his* Christ, and the dead shall be revived."

This reference to the return of those who dwell under the shadow of Almighty God will have a dual fulfillment. There is here a meaningful allusion to the actual resurrection from the grave of those who will arise to assume rulership with Jesus Christ in the restored Kingdom. But this is also a reference to the resurrection of the House of Israel from the graveyard of Assyrian captivity because God said, "I will ransom them from the power of the grave; I will redeem them from death" (Hosea 13: 14). To ransom means to redeem by paying a price, referring to those for whom a price was paid down to redeem them from bondage and death. Beholding in vision the glorious return of the triumphant remnant who gather at the seat of His government (Zion) and rally about the throne of the Kingdom, Isaiah exclaimed:

> "And the ransomed of the Lord shall return, and come to Zion with songs and everlasting joy upon their heads: they shall obtain joy and gladness, and sorrow and sighing shall flee away." (Isa. 35: 10; see also Isa. 51: 11.)

The Prophet Hosea goes on to assert that His people shall "revive as the corn" and the comment upon this statement by Dr. Adam Clarke is informative and invaluable:

> "The justness and beauty of this metaphor is not generally perceived. After the corn has been a short time above the earth, in a single spike, the blades begin to separate, and the stalk to spring out of the center. The side leaves turn back to make way for the protruding stalk; and fall, bending down to the earth, assuming a withered appearance, though still attached to the plant. To look at the corn in this state, no one, unacquainted with the circumstances, could entertain any sanguine hope of a copious harvest. In a short time other leaves spring out; the former freshen, and begin to stand erect; *and the whole seems to revive from a vegetative death.* This is the circumstance to which the prophet refers." (*Clarke's Commentary,* Vol. IV, p. 654.)

Therefore, the prophet says that Israel (those dwelling under His shadow) shall return; they shall revive; they shall grow. Speaking of the full restoration of the Kingdom, the prophet continues, "The scent thereof [as of blossoms, with the rich promise of fruit] shall be as the wine of Lebanon."

GLORY AND GREATNESS OF THE KINGDOM

The future greatness of His Kingdom people will only be predicated upon the fact that the Glory of the Lord will be seen among them:

"Arise, shine; for thy light is come, and the glory of the Lord is risen upon thee." (Isa. 60: 1.)

The prophet describes the effect of the exaltation of the Kingdom, with the Holy One of Israel dwelling in the midst of the people:

"For the nation and kingdom that will not serve thee shall perish; yea, those nations shall be utterly wasted." (Isa. 60: 12.)

Of those who had oppressed His people in the past, Isaiah declares:

"The sons also of them that afflicted thee shall come bending unto thee; and all they that despised thee shall bow themselves down at the soles of thy feet." (Isa. 60: 14.)

Peace and prosperity, with the elimination of all violence and crime, are promised to Israel in the glorious Kingdom age:

"I will make thee an eternal excellency, a joy of many generations. . . . I will also make thy officers peace, and thine exactors righteousness. Violence shall no more be heard in thy land, wasting nor destruction within thy borders; but thou shalt call thy walls Salvation, and thy gates Praise. . . . The Lord shall be thine everlasting light, and the days of thy mourning shall be ended. Thy people also shall be all righteous: they shall inherit the land for ever, the branch of my planting, the work of my hands, that I may be glorified. . . . I the Lord will hasten it in his time." (Isa. 60: 15-22.)

The nations will behold the coming of the King in all His glory when He takes the throne of His father David and prepares to reign over the House of Jacob forever. Then the prophecy will be fulfilled:

"The mountain [Kingdom] of the house of the Lord shall be established in the top of the mountains [high above all kingdoms], and it shall be exalted above the hills [governments]; and people shall flow unto it. And many nations shall come, and say, Come, and let us go up to the mountain [Kingdom] of the Lord, and to the house [or Temple] of the God of Jacob; and he will teach us of his ways, and we will walk in his paths: for the law shall go forth of Zion [the seat of His government], and the word of the Lord from Jerusalem [the ecclesiastical center of worship]. And he [Jesus Christ, the King] shall judge among many people, and rebuke strong nations afar off; and they shall beat their swords into plowshares, and their spears into pruninghooks: nation shall not lift up a sword against nation, neither shall they learn war any more." (Micah 4: 1-3.)

A Divine Proclamation

The prophecies of Isaiah are replete with picturesque descriptions of the exalted position the nations of Israel will occupy when God's purposes are carried out in their entirety. He was led to exclaim:

"Thou shalt also be a crown of glory in the hand of the Lord, and a royal diadem in the hand of thy God. Thou shalt no more be termed Forsaken; neither shall thy land any more be termed Desolate: but thou shalt be called Hephzibah [my delight is in her], and thy land Beulah [married]: for the Lord delighteth in thee, and thy land shall be married." (Isa. 62: 3-4.)

Every Divine assurance has been given that these prophecies will be fulfilled, but the Lord suggests, nevertheless, the part consecrated ones among His people are to play:

"I have set watchmen upon thy walls, O Jerusalem, which shall never hold their peace day nor night: ye that make mention of the Lord, keep not silence, and give him no rest, till he establish, and till he make Jerusalem a praise in the earth." (Isa. 62: 6-7.)

The Lord's love for His Holy City, Jerusalem, is manifested throughout the Scriptures and the Psalmist counseled:

"Pray for the peace of Jerusalem: they shall prosper that love thee." (Ps. 122: 6.)

If those, therefore, who are in a position to "make mention of the Lord" will beseech Him in prayer to fulfill the promises in His Word, and "give Him no rest" until He does so, as He Himself invites us to do, nothing can prevent the complete restoration of the Kingdom of God on earth, with Jerusalem as its glorious capital. That the zeal of the Lord of Hosts will accomplish this is firmly assured by His own proclamation:

"Behold, the Lord hath proclaimed unto the end of the world, Say ye to the daughter of Zion, Behold, thy salvation cometh; behold, his reward is with him, and his work before him. And they shall call them, The holy people, The redeemed of the Lord: and thou shalt be called, Sought out, A city not forsaken." (Isa. 62: 11-12.)

This was preceded by the voice of the crier, heralding the return of the royal race:

"Go through, go through the gates; prepare ye the way of the people; cast up, cast up the highway; gather out the stones; lift up a standard for the people." (Isa. 62: 10.)

Hosea shows that the House of Israel will have become so convinced of the goodness of the Lord when they behold the outcome of His might and power in their defense against their enemies that all their former idolatrous thoughts, attributing their prosperity to sources other than their God, will become abhorrent to them. The idol worship of past generations will vanish from among them:

"Ephraim shall say, What have I to do any more with idols? I have heard him, and observed him: I am like a green fir tree. From me is thy fruit found." (Hosea 14: 8.)

The final conversion of the people and leadership of the nations of Israel will be sincere and complete. With utter satisfaction and contentment, the people will affirm, "I am like a green fir tree," knowing that the words of the Lord are true: "From me is thy fruit found." In the closing verse of his book the Prophet Hosea confirms the justice and infinite mercy of God's ways: "Who is wise, and he shall understand these things? Prudent, and he shall know them? For the ways of the Lord are right, and the just shall walk in them: but the transgressors shall fall therein."

Index

Aaronic Order, 74
Abel, 5
Abraham
  Covenant promise to, 9
  Their father, 52
Acceptable Time, 31, 36, 45
  Beginning of, 35
Acceptable Year, 38
Achor
  Meaning of, 34
  Valley of, 33
Admah, 116
Adultery, 70
Ahab, 6, 16
Ahaz, 1
Almighty God
  Shadow of, 142
Amalekites, 137
America
  Colonization of, 45, 51, 89
Ammi, 20, 57
  My people, 17
Ancient Order
  Of Master Shepherds, 13
Anglo-Saxon-Celtic Peoples, 11, 45, 52, 63, 106, 133
  Expansion of, 89
Anglo-Saxon-Celtic World, 52
Anglo-Saxondom
  Sins of, 108
  Superficial supplications, 104
Apostasy
  General, 79
  The great, 70
Apostate Children, 79
Apostolic Descent
  Not sustained, 63
Appointed Place, 10, 61, 68, 89
Ark of the Covenant, 5
Asia
  Out of, 66
Asiatics
  And aggressions, 104
Asshur
  Not save us, 136
Assyria
  Carried away into, 18
  Israel left, 130
  Israel subject to, 109
  The death-land, 127
Assyrian
  Became their king, 115

Assyrian Captivity, 21, 61, 143
  Bondage in, 116
  Escape from, 10
  Israel carried into, 8, 29, 31
  Israel cast away into, 111
  Israel moved out of, 33
  Strangulation in, 124
Assyrian Grave, 128
Assyrian Graveyard, 126
Assyrian Invasion, 69
Assyrians
  Israel's oppressors, 120
  Turned to, 84
Augustine, 64
Avenger of Blood, 96, 97

Baal
  Attributing prosperity to, 27
  Futility of serving, 26
  Israel served, 50
  No longer refer to, 46
  To serve, 57
  Worship licentious, 16
Baalim
  Days of, 27, 51
Baalism
  Idolatrous worship of, 19
Baal-peor, 111
Baals
  Her lovers, 19
Baal Worship, 16
Babylon
  Apostle to, 63
Babylonian Captivity, 21
Baxter, William J., 71
Benjamin
  Most of tribe destroyed, 111
  Punishment overtook, 81
Beth-aven, 82
Bethel, 82, 98
Betrothed
  In righteousness, 53
Bible
  Portrays great changes, 72
  Translated, 44
Bible References
  (see Scriptural Texts)
Black Sea, 67
British Commonwealth, 133
British Isles, 50, 133

Christian Church in, 63
Brutus
  Of Troy, 65
Building and Planting, 67

Calves
  Of our lips, 136
Caspian Sea, 67
Caucasus
  Gateway of, 68
Caucasus Mountains, 66
Chemivision, 23
Childbirth
  Analogy of, 124
Christian
  Ignorant of God's plans, 95
  In their songs, 11
  Knows little of Bible, 70
Christian Church
  The first, 64
Christian Circumcision, 10
Christian Dispensation, 69
  High Priest in, 97
Christianity
  Not by way of Rome, 64
  Originated in Palestine, 63
  Rome's claim to, 63
  Took root, 46
  True seat of, 65
Christian People, 62
  Israel as a, 23
Circumcision
  Christian, 10
Cities of Refuge, 96
City
  Not enter into, 116
Civilization
  A new, 45
Clarke, Dr. Adam, 143
Clarke's Commentary, 143
Colonial Expansion, 44
Communist China, 101
Covenant
  Bond of, 24
  Breaking the, 95
  If clauses, 50
  Keep terms of, 103
  New, 9, 37, 140
  Of peace, 49, 50
  Of their ancestors, 31
  Penalties for violation, 25
  With the beasts, 48

149

Creation
No discord throughout, 54
Crier
Voice of, 147
Crime
Elimination of, 144
On the increase, 70
Cursing, 70
Cyprus, 101

Dates, A.D.
597 A.D., 64
686 A.D., 64
1001-2 A.D., 88
1066 A.D., 88
1551-1552 A.D., 50
1601-1668 A.D., 51
1800-1802 A.D., 51
2001-2 A.D., 88
Dates, A.M.
3000 A.M., 88
3996 A.M., 88
5000 A.M., 88
6000 A.M., 88
Dates, B.C.
4-3 B.C., 88
721 B.C., 27, 28, 62
914-853 B.C., 89
1000-999 B.C., 88
1486 B.C., 27
David
Covenant with, 68
Throne of, 145
Davidic Monarch
Awaiting their coming, 66
Day of Salvation, 36
Days
Week of, 87
Dead
Awakening of, 55
Be revived, 142
Life from, 140, 141
Sown in earth, 56
Death
Cases of accidental, 96
Redeem from, 143
Death-land, 127
Delitzsch, 78
Diblaim, 4
Divorce, 118, 139
Cut off from God by, 130
Divorcement
Bill of, 20, 21, 23, 31
Doctors, 74
Drought, 71
Dry Bones
Ezekiel's vision, 132
Filling a valley, 23
Dust
Sleep in, 55

Earth
Sown in, 56
Eastminster, 64
Ebbsfleet, 64
Eber, 5
Egypt
Cruel bondage in, 109
Ephraim sending oil into, 120
Some fled to, 109
Son called out of, 114
Egyptian Cavalry, 137

Elect
For sake of, 117
Elijah, 2, 16, 40
Felt he alone left, 18
Elijah's Altar
Fire of God upon, 16
Elisha, 2
Elizabeth I, 45
Elizabethan Period, 45
Ephraim
Birthright tribe, 109
Broken in judgment, 83
Decline of, 100
Guilt of, 98
Ignored word of the Lord, 107
Iniquity of, 124
Judgment pronounced upon, 76
Lord's quarrel with, 120
Meek and humble, 122
Ethbaal, 16
Ethelbert
Time of King, 65
Europe
Wilderness of, 61, 68

False Pastors, 11
False Prophets, 5
First Resurrection, 141
Foreign Alliances, 102
Foreign Alliances Condemned, 101
Fullness of the Ages
Dispensation of, 88

Gate
Passed through, 66, 67
Generation
A sinful, 69
Generations
Check spirituality, 73
Gentiles
Benefited by fall, 139
Gibeah, 81
Gibraltar, 101
Glastonbury, England, 63
God
Abandoned His people, 76
Answer to prayer, 138
Appeal to, 86
Becomes the Adversary, 85
End of patience, 71
House of, 82
Kingdom of, 49
Kings not selected by, 105
Knowledge essential, 94
Living in His sight, 90
Pronounces judgment, 11
Proper approach to, 135
Rejected Israel, 75
Return to Him, 86
Ruling with, 119
Sons of, 9, 11
Superficial worship of, 93
Gods
Desire to exchange, 26
God Sows, 56

God's People
All righteous, 54
Gog, 141
Of the land of Magog, 87
Golden Calf, 82, 98
Pronounced judgment upon, 105
Gomer, 4, 5, 7
Weaned Lo-ruhamah, 8
Gomorrah, 116
Goshen
Land of, 115
Gospel of Salvation
Message of, 64
Seeds of, 65
Gozan
River of, 28
Gracious One, 136
Grave
An unmarked, 126
Of forgetfulness, 129, 141
Place of forgetfulness, 126
Ransomed from, 133
Resurrection from, 127, 143
Graves
Arisen from, 57
Graveyard
A spiritual, 127
Assyria, 126, 143
Great Army
An exceeding, 133
Great Britain
Wasting away, 100
Great Captivity
Beginning of, 28
Great Day
Of Jezreel, 55

Habor, 28
Halah, 28
Hale, William J., 23, 61
Harvest
God's, 14
Great day of, 55
Time of, 98
Hawaiian Islands, 35
Heathen
Abominations of, 79
Become like, 24
Heber, 5
Hezekiah, 1
Higher Criticism and the Monuments, 84
Holy Spirit
Guiding power of, 114
Hosea
Commission of, 2
First child, 5
Marriage of, 4
Married an idolatress, 3
Told to marry, 59
To marry a wife, 17
Hoshea
Reign as king, 28
House of David, 4
Transfer of, 67
House of Israel, 2, 4, 7, 16, 53, 60, 63, 65
Apostatized, 3
As sand of sea, 133
Called to return, 135
Christianized, 9, 69

Convinced of God's goodness, 147
Divorced, 20, 139
Dry bones, 129, 131
Ephraim Israel, 132
Escape penalty of law, 22
Fear the Lord, 69
Find grace, 10
Found grace, 44
From the grave, 127
Great apostasy of, 70
Leadership in Ephraim, 119
Live again in God's sight, 127
Lord had divorced, 24
Lost all contact, 126
Lost sheep of, 13, 64
Message sent to, 37
Modern, 8
No mercy upon, 57
Provoked the Lord, 122
Receive the Kingdom, 131
Redemption of, 133
Reduced to poverty, 26
Refused to return, 84
Refuses to heed, 19
Restoration from death, 141
Restoration of, 58
Return of, 138
Ruling over, 68
Seven thousand faithful, 18
Told set free, 37
Turned to idolatry, 24
Under curse of law, 43
Unfaithful wife, 125
Without a king, 66
House of Judah
Reassured of mercy, 7

Idolatrous Practices, 95
Idolatry
Bred faithlessness, 4
Freed from, 45
No longer practiced, 62
Repudiation of, 137
Idols
Credit to, 123
Kissed the, 122
Silver and gold made into, 105
Worshipping, 17
Idol Worship
Vanish from Israel, 147
Images
Removed, 50
Immanuel, 46
Indictment
Ready, 124
Intoxication, 99
Isaac
Covenant promise to, 9
Ishi
Meaning of, 46
Isles
Of the sea, 65, 133
People in, 69
Israel
About to awaken, 86
Apostasy in, 93
Appoints one head, 14
A select planting, 56

Base sins of, 121
Became not His people, 20
Being allured, 33
Betrothed to God, 52
Blindness of, 139
Called out of Egypt, 114
Carried away captive, 88
Christianized, 23
Coming to himself, 139
Company of nations, 90
Covenant made with, 95
Daughters of, 16
Divorced, 38
Divorced mother, 138
Dwelling in the wilderness, 132
Dwelt in the wilderness, 107
Eventually restored, 61
Expansion of, 43
Expansion of modern, 89
Forbidden agreements, 112
Forced into Assyrian captivity, 104
Forgot their Maker, 110
God called, 63
Held laws in contempt, 109
Holy One of, 144
House of, 52, 58
Inability to extricate herself, 39
In her grave, 129
In the Isles, 119
Like an empty vine, 111
Moral and spiritual degeneration, 98
Must awaken, 90
No longer remembered gods, 47
No longer stand before enemies, 105
Parenthood in, 80
Prayer to pray, 138
Priestly functions, 74
Receive Gospel, 88
Redeemer of, 140
Refusing to be led, 76
Repudiated as administrators, 74
Restoration of, 108
Sacrifices not save them, 79
Seek the Lord, 77
Shall know, 110
Sin of modern, 85
Spiritual reawakening, 141
Swallowed up, 106
The pride of, 101
The wife repudiated, 18
Tidings of redemption to, 63
Two ways before her, 103
Word light upon, 132
Word taken to, 133
Israel and Judah

Not same people, 21
Israel's Fall, 139
Israel-Syrian Wars, 89

Jacob
Covenant promise to, 9
House of, 145
Unconverted name, 121
Word sent into, 46, 132
Jareb
King of Assyria, 84
Jehu, 6
House of, 6
Jeremiah
Wards of, 68
Jeroboam, 1, 4, 6
Idolatrous practices of, 83
Jerusalem, 4
Escaped, 8
Glorious capital, 146
God's love for, 146
Jesus Christ
Acceptance of, 14
Appointed Head, 12
As Redeemer, 66, 136
Commissioned His disciples, 64
High Priest prefigured, 97
In day of His power, 15
In Egypt, 114
Jews reject, 131
Lion of Judah, 118
Master Shepherd, 12
Messiah, 11
Nullified bill of divorcement, 37
Redeeming love of, 69
Resurrection of, 133
Return of, 91
Rulership with, 143
Shadow of, 142
The Testator, 140
To pay the ransom, 127
Triumphant return, 118
Word made flesh, 46, 132
Jews
Did not respond, 39
Do not fill conditions, 11
Not accept Jesus Christ, 131
Refused to receive Him, 132
Jezebel, 6
Wife of Ahab, 16
Jezreel, 55
Blood of, 6
Day of, 13
Son of Hosea, 5
They shall hear, 56
Joash, 1
Joel, 1
Jonah, 1
Joseph
Mary and, 114
Joseph of Arimathea, 63, 64
Jotham, 1
Judah
Appoints one head, 14
Built fortified cities, 110

Lion of, 119
Not divorced, 20, 38, 139
Return to Palestine, 21
Stumbled, 79
Taken to Babylon, 88
Turned away from God, 120
Warned, 76
Judah and Israel
Contrast between, 8
Judgment
Certainty of, 110
Coming desolation, 83
Day of, 13
Indicator of, 71
On the earth, 72
Prelude to, 72
Visitation of, 73
Juvenile Delinquency, 70, 99

King
God had given, 123
Pass on before them, 66
Preceded by, 66
Kingdom of God, 49, 74
Citizens of, 81
Custodianship of, 131
Disaster overtook, 124
Exalted above all governments, 124
Gospel of, 131
Greatness of, 144
Leadership in, 55
Nucleus of, 125
Power died a-borning, 124
Restoration of, 58, 146
Taken from Jews, 64
Thrones in, 55
Transferred, 37
King of Kings
Lord of lords, 124

Latter Days, 68
Law
Curse of, 22, 130
Of Divorcement, 20
Law of the Lord
Administration of, 57, 75, 124
Laws
Must restore, 53
Lawyers, 74
Leagues
And agreements, 137
Lebanon
Wine of, 144
Leopard
Wait for prey, 123
Levitical Order, 74
Lightbearers, 64
Lion
Of Tribe of Judah, 118
Roars, 118
Wait for prey, 123
Lips
Sacrifices of, 136
Lo
Prefix dropped, 17
Lo-ammi, 17, 57, 139
London
First bishop of, 65
First Church in, 64

Paul visited, 63
Lord
Betraying the, 80
Day of, 14
His ways are right, 147
Lack of knowledge of, 70
Law of, 53
Return unto, 90
Will be Israel's king, 123
Lord of Lords
King of kings, 124
Lo-ruhamah, 7, 17, 57
Lucives, 64
Lying, 70

Magog, 141
Mammon
Serve God and, 111
Master Shepherd
Jesus Christ, 12
Medes
Cities of, 28
Melchisedec
Order of, 97
Meshech
Chief prince of, 87
Messiah
God will vindicate, 41
Greatness of, 43
Speaks, 39
States source of help, 40
Title of, 136
Military Might
Inadequacy of, 113
Millennial Rest, 88
Millennial Rule, 88
Millet
A monk, 65
Missionary Activities, 90
Missionary Movements, 52
Mizpah
Meaning of, 78
Modernism
Leadership of, 11
Modernists, 79
Moscow, 87
Moses, 40
Mount of Transfiguration, 40
Mount Sinai, 53, 74, 95
Murder, 70
Readily committed, 99

Naguib, 100
Napoleon
Defeated, 51
Nehru, 100
New Covenant
Sealed terms of, 37
Nineveh, 84
Norman Conquest, 88, 89
North American Continent, 34, 35

Order of Melchisedec, 97
Orphaned Children, 138

Palestine
Isles north and west of, 35
North and west of, 45
Papacy

Center of, 63
Parents
Responsibility of, 81
Parturition
Crisis in, 124
Peace
And prosperity, 144
Covenant of, 49, 50
Demonstration of, 75
Peleg, 5
Peter
Never in Rome, 63
Philadelphia
One of seven churches, 52
Pope
Before first, 63
Pope Gregory
The Great, 64
Prayer
Israel to pray, 135, 138
Joel's, 86
Prayers
Not heard, 79
Priest
Defined, 74
High, 96
Priesthood
Corrupt, 97
Priestly Office
Biblical definition, 74
Priests
Condemned, 78
Failure of, 76
Profiting by murder, 97
Proclamation
A Divine, 145
Prodigal
Returns, 138
Prophets
Failure of, 76
Foolish, 110
School of, 1
Prosperity
Destruction of, 26
Punishment
Rod of, 25
Puritan Movement, 51, 89

Raisin-cakes, 60
Ramah
Blowing trumpet in, 82
Ramoth-Gilead, 96, 98
Rebellion
Compounded, 103
Final act of, 106
Rebetrothal
Steps in, 51
Redeemer, 22, 118
And Saviour, 119
Came to His own, 39
Redemption, 36
Certainty of, 42
Reformation, 44, 90
Rehoboam
Revolted from rule of, 27
Repentance
Call to, 113
Or judgment, 117
Restoration
Full, 47, 48, 144
Of Israel, 108
Of prosperity, 91
Time of, 14, 91
Resurrected Ones, 56

Resurrection, 55
  A national, 128
  Purpose of, 128
  The First, 141
Righteousness
  Betrothed in, 53
  Fill earth with, 124
  Harvest of, 56
  Ignoring standards of,
    121
  Restore, 91
Righteous People, 53
Rome
  Paul in, 63
  Peter never in, 63
Ruhamah, 20
  Having obtained morcy,
    17

St. Avstin
  The Apostle, 65
St. Peter Upon-Cornhill
  Church of, 64, 65
Salvation, 36
  Day of, 36
  For all mankind, 139
  Gospel of, 90
Samaria, 84
  Captured by Assyrians,
    114
  Capture of, 28
  Fall of, 1
  Following east wind,
    120
  Gentiles encamped
    against, 7
  King cut off, 112
  Sin of, 98
  Taken, 28
Sarah
  Their mother, 52
Sargon II, 84
Sayce, Professor, 84
Scriptural Texts
Genesis
  10: 25, p. 5
  19: 1-13, p. 116
  24: 60, p. 100
  48: 19, p. 134
Exodus
  19: 5-6, p. 74
  19: 8, p. 53
  20: 13, p. 96
  23: 32, pp. 84, 137
  23: 32-33, p. 102
Leviticus
  26, p. 103
  26: 4-5, p. 54
  26: 27-28, p. 28
  26: 44-45, p. 31
Numbers
  35, p. 96
Deuteronomy
  4: 5-8, p. 75
  6: 1-7, p. 81
  19: 14, p. 83
  24: 1-4, pp. 20, 140
  25: 13-16, p. 121
  28, p. 103
  28: 33, p. 83
  32: 8, p. 34
  34: 7, p. 102
Joshua
  7: 20-26, p. 34
  9, p. 112
  21: 38, p. 96

Judges
  19-21, p. 111
I Samuel
  4: 22, p. 5
  15: 23, p. 137
II Samuel
  7: 10, pp. 61, 89
I Kings
  12: 29, p. 82
  13: 1-10, p. 5
  18: 39, p. 16
  19: 18, p. 18
II Kings
  10: 30, p. 6
  17: 6-23, p. 106
  17: 7-18, p. 29
Psalms
  6: 5, p. 126
  44: 11, p. 130
  50: 14-15, p. 136
  91, p. 142
  91: 1, p. 142
  122: 6, p. 146
Ecclesiastes
  9: 10, p. 126
Isaiah
  2: 2, p. 49
  2: 2-3, p. 124
  9: 6-7, pp. 46, 132
  9: 8, p. 46
  9: 8-9, p. 132
  11: 6-9, p. 48
  26: 19, pp. 14, 55
  35: 10, p. 143
  41: 1, pp. 89, 107
  49: 8, pp. 35, 36
  49: 12, p. 34
  50: 1, p. 38
  50: 2, p. 39
  50: 4, p. 40
  50: 5, p. 40
  50: 6, p. 40
  50: 7, p. 40
  51, p. 42
  51: 1, p. 41
  51: 1-2, pp. 10, 52
  51: 11, p. 143
  51: 22-23, p. 42
  52, p. 42
  52: 3, p. 42
  52: 13-15, p. 42
  53, p. 43
  53: 1, p. 43
  53: 5-6, p. 43
  54: 1, p. 43
  54: 2-4, p. 44
  54: 5, p. 18
  54: 5-6, p. 32
  54: 7-8, p. 32
  56: 1, p. 53
  60: 1, pp. 90, 144
  60: 12, p. 144
  60: 14, p. 144
  60: 15-22, p. 145
  60: 17-18 & 20, p. 57
  60: 21, p. 54
  61: 2, p. 36
  62: 3-4, p. 146
  62: 6-7, p. 146
  62: 10, p. 147
  62: 11-12, p. 146
Jeremiah
  1: 10, p. 67
  3: 8, pp. 21, 120
  23: 2-6, p. 12
  23: 10, p. 71

  23: 11, p. 76
  30: 16-17, p. 90
  31: 1, p. 132
  31: 2, pp. 10, 44, 132
  31: 31-33, p. 38
  31: 32, p. 125
  33: 17, p. 68
Ezekiel
  20: 30-31, p. 24
  20: 32, p. 24
  20: 33-37, p. 25
  20: 35, p. 130
  20: 35-36, p. 32
  34: 22-23, p. 12
  34: 23-25, p. 49
  36: 27, p. 53
  36: 33-38, p. 22
  37: 1-10, p. 129
  37: 4, p. 131
  37: 10, p. 133
  37: 11, pp. 24, 130
  37: 12-14, p. 141
  38, p. 87
  39, p. 87
  39: 21-29, p. 142
Daniel
  12: 2, p. 14
Hosea
  1: 1, p. 1
  1: 2, p. 2
  1: 3, p. 4
  1: 4, p. 6
  1: 6, p. 7
  1: 7, p. 7
  1: 9, pp. 8, 139
  1: 10, pp. 9, 62, 66,
    133, 140
  1: 11, pp. 11, 13, 14
  2: 1-2, p. 17
  2: 3, p. 19
  2: 4-5, p. 19
  2: 6-7, p. 25
  2: 9-10, p. 26
  2: 11-12, p. 27
  2: 13, p. 27
  2: 14, p. 32
  2: 15, p. 34
  2: 16, p. 46
  2: 17, p. 47
  2: 18, p. 49
  2: 19-20, p. 51
  2: 21-22, pp. 54, 55
  2: 23, p. 56
  3: 1, p. 59
  3: 3, p. 60
  3: 4, pp. 61, 107, 130
  3: 5, pp. 62, 69, 107
  4: 1, p. 69
  4: 2, p. 70
  4: 3, p. 71
  4: 6, pp. 74, 75
  4: 9-10, p. 76
  4: 17, p. 76
  5: 1, p. 78
  5: 2, p. 78
  5: 7, p. 80
  5: 8, p. 82
  5: 12, pp. 83, 84
  5: 13, p. 85
  5: 14-15, p. 85
  6: 1, pp. 90, 93
  6: 1-3, p. 86
  6: 2, p. 90
  6: 3, pp. 90, 91
  6: 4, p. 93
  6: 5-6, p. 94

6: 7, p. 95
6: 8-9, p. 97
6: 9, p. 97
6: 10-11, p. 98
7: 1-2, pp. 98, 99
7: 8, p. 102
7: 8-10, p. 100
7: 9, p. 101
7: 11, p. 101
7: 12, p. 102
7: 13-14, p. 103
7: 15-16, p. 104
8: 1, p. 105
8: 2, p. 105
8: 3, p. 105
8: 7, p. 105
8: 8, p. 106
8: 9-10, p. 107
8: 10, p. 107
8: 13-14, p. 109
9: 3, p. 110
9: 7, p. 110
9: 17, p. 111
10: 3-4, p. 112
10: 6, p. 84
10: 7, p. 112
10: 12, p. 113
10: 13, p. 113
10: 14, p. 113
10: 15, p. 114
11: 1, p. 114
11: 5, p. 115
11: 8, p. 116
11: 9, p. 116
11: 10, p. 118
11: 12, p. 119
12: 1, p. 120
12: 6, p. 121
12: 7, p. 121
12: 8, p. 121
12: 9, p. 122
12: 12, p. 124
12: 13, p. 122
12: 15, p. 122
13: 1, p. 122
13: 2, p. 123
13: 3, p. 123
13: 4, p. 123
13: 9-10, p. 123
13: 13, p. 124
13: 14, pp. 126, 127,
    128, 143
14: 1, p. 135
14: 1-3, p. 137
14: 2, p. 135
14: 2-3, p. 136
14: 4-6, p. 138
14: 7, p. 142
14: 8, p. 147
Joel
2: 16-17, p. 87
2: 17, p. 138
2: 18-27, p. 138
2: 19, p. 55
2: 20-23, p. 91
Amos
9: 9, p. 134
Micah
2: 13, p. 66
4: 1, p. 49
4: 1-3, p. 145
4: 2, pp. 49, 50
4: 3, p. 50
Habakkuk
1: 13, p. 117
Zephaniah

3: 13-20, p. 23
Zechariah
8: 8, p. 58
8: 12, p. 58
13: 9, p. 58
Malachi
3: 17-18, p. 57
Matthew
2: 15, p. 114
10: 5-7, pp. 13, 37,
    131
10: 6, p. 119
13: 41, p. 14
15: 14, p. 78
21: 43, pp. 65, 131
23: 38, p. 131
24: 22, p. 117
Luke
4: 18-19, p. 36
9: 30-31, p. 41
9: 51, p. 41
15: 11-32, p. 139
John
1: 11, pp. 39, 132
1: 14, pp. 46, 132
10: 14-15, p. 13
10: 17-18, p. 41
Acts
3: 19, p. 92
Romans
2: 29, p. 10
7: 1-2, p. 22
9: 25, p. 7
11: 11-15, p. 139
11: 15, p. 140
11: 32, p. 140
I Corinthians
15, p. 128
15: 41-44 & 52, p. 56
15: 54-55, p. 128
II Corinthians
6: 2, p. 38
Hebrews
6: 20, p. 97
8: 8-12, p. 37
9: 14-17, p. 140
I Peter
2: 10, p. 7
5: 13, p. 63
II Peter
3: 8, p. 87
Revelation
3: 7-8, p. 52
19: 7, p. 140
20: 6, p. 55
II Esdras
13: 40-45, pp. 33, 67
13: 40-46, p. 131
Sea
Isles of, 50
Seth, 5
Seven Thousand
Not bowed knees, 18
Seven Times, 28, 50, 51,
    89
Of punishment, 28
Shalmaneser, 84
Shepherds
In Israel, 11
Sinai, 53
Slave
Redemption of, 60
Sodom, 116
Solomon
Let astray, 27
Soviet Russia, 101

Agreements with, 86
Fulfilling predictions,
    87
Spanish Armada, 45
Spiritual Understanding
At lowest ebb, 70
Stubbornness
Form of idolatry, 137
Suez Canal, 101
Swearing
The stream of, 70

Targum, 142
Tax Collectors, 74
Theft, 70
Throne of David
Transported, 68
Time
Process of, 50
Today's Revolution in
Weather, 71
Transfiguration
Mount of, 40
Tribulation
Days to be shortened,
    117

United States, 34, 133
Unrighteous Practices
Turn from, 73
Uzziah, 1

Valley
Dry bones scattered
over, 130
Valley of Achor, 33
Valley of Dry Bones, 129,
    131
Violence
Elimination of, 144
Vows
Restatement of, 58

Wars
Will cease, 49
Weather
Revolution in, 72
Week of Days, 87
Westminster, 64
Westward Trek, 23
Beginning of, 35
Wife
Divorced, 42
Of whoredoms, 3
Wilderness
Grace in, 132
Israel sing in, 44
Of the people, 32, 130
Territory designated,
    34
William the Conqueror,
    88
Woman
Hosea purchased, 60
World War II, 86

Years
360 years, 28, 50
1,000 years, 88
2,520 years, 28, 89

Zeboim, 116
Zedekiah
Daughters of, 68
Zidonians
King of, 16

FOR the first time a book has appeared that provides a complete exposition of the writings of the Prophet Hosea, the best known of the minor prophets. All the vital truths pertaining to God's plan concerning His Kingdom and its future greatness are presented in full detail in *Study in Hosea*. Those seeking a clearly-stated definition of terms in relation to the people of His Kingdom will discover that this book contains the exegesis that will help them most. It will also meet the requirements of those looking for a fundamental treatise explaining basic Scriptural facts.

While Hosea is numbered among the minor prophets because of the brevity of his book in the Bible, its message is by no means secondary in importance. In graphic, sometimes symbolic, terms Hosea tells the story of the rejection, the punishment, the regathering and the ultimate restoration of the House of Israel. In one bold sweep across the centuries, beginning with the dispersion of the House of Israel and climaxing in their redemption, the resurrection of their rulers and the restoration of the Kingdom, followed by universal peace and prosperity, the prophet provides a telescopic preview of the march of the House of Israel down through the pages of history.

This prophet clearly sets forth the distinction between Israel and Judah and justifies God's dealings with His people

(Continued on back flap)